Your Guide to Successful Postgraduate Study

Sara Miller McCune founded SAGE Publishing in 1965 to support the dissemination of usable knowledge and educate a global community. SAGE publishes more than 1000 journals and over 800 new books each year, spanning a wide range of subject areas. Our growing selection of library products includes archives, data, case studies and video. SAGE remains majority owned by our founder and after her lifetime will become owned by a charitable trust that secures the company's continued independence.

Los Angeles | London | New Delhi | Singapore | Washington DC | Melbourne

→SAGE Study Skills

Your Guide to Successful Postgraduate Study

Geoffrey Elliott,
Karima Kadi-Hanifi &
Carla Solvason

$SAGE

Los Angeles | London | New Delhi
Singapore | Washington DC | Melbourne

Los Angeles | London | New Delhi
Singapore | Washington DC | Melbourne

SAGE Publications Ltd
1 Oliver's Yard
55 City Road
London EC1Y 1SP

SAGE Publications Inc.
2455 Teller Road
Thousand Oaks, California 91320

SAGE Publications India Pvt Ltd
B 1/I 1 Mohan Cooperative Industrial Area
Mathura Road
New Delhi 110 044

SAGE Publications Asia-Pacific Pte Ltd
3 Church Street
#10-04 Samsung Hub
Singapore 049483

Editor: Jude Bowen
Editorial assistant: Catriona McMullen
Production editor: Nicola Carrier
Proofreader: Audrey Scriven
Indexer: Author
Marketing manager: Lorna Patkai
Cover design: Sheila Tong
Typeset by: C&M Digitals (P) Ltd, Chennai, India
Printed in the UK

Library of Congress Control Number: 2017949625

British Library Cataloguing in Publication data

A catalogue record for this book is available from the British Library

ISBN 978-1-5264-1128-0
ISBN 978-1-5264-1129-7 (pbk)

At SAGE we take sustainability seriously. Most of our products are printed in the UK using responsibly sourced papers and boards. When we print overseas we ensure sustainable papers are used as measured by the PREPS grading system. We undertake an annual audit to monitor our sustainability.

Contents

List of Drawings, Figures and Tables   vi

About the Authors   vii

Acknowledgements   ix

Introduction   1

1 Understanding Yourself as a Learner and Postgraduate Student   3

2 The Study Environment   15

3 The Unspoken Rules of Academic Etiquette   29

4 Reading to Some Purpose   43

5 The Representation of Thinking at Postgraduate Level   56

6 The Postgraduate-Level Linguistic Skills   71

7 Preparing Your Dissertation or Thesis Proposal   88

8 Next Steps   106

References   125

Index   126

List of Drawings, Figures and Tables

Drawings

1.1   Tree   10

2.1   Pocket Book of Answers   19

3.1   Do *not* disturb   31

4.1   Reading in bed   46

5.1   Re-present machine   59

6.1   Final final final *draft*   75

7.1   Running against four clocks   101

8.1   Doing personal development planning   116

Figure

6.1   English for academic purposes (EAP): A hierarchical functional engine   84

Tables

2.1   Typical fees for a UK student applying for a one-year full-time Master's course – 180 Master's (M) level Credits – or a PhD, 2017   23

2.2   Examples of part-time annual course fees set pro rata to the full-time fee   24

About the Authors

Geoffrey Elliott is Professor of Post-Compulsory Education at the University of Worcester. He has worked in schools, further and adult education, and has previously held posts at the School of Independent Study at the University of East London, and the Open University where he taught on the Professional Doctorate programme in Education. His research interests are in Leadership, Ethics and Widening Participation in Higher Education. Geoffrey is President of the Association for Research in Post-Compulsory Education, the sponsor of the international peer-reviewed journal *Research in Post-Compulsory Education*, which he has edited since its launch in 1996. He has written and co-authored a number of books, including (with Carol Costley and Paul Gibbs) the highly popular *Doing Work Based Research: Approaches to Enquiry for Insider-Researchers* (Sage, 2010). Geoffrey is currently a member of the Board of Directors of the Office of the Independent Adjudicator for Higher Education (OIA), the complaints ombudsman for higher education (HE) students studying in England and Wales.

Karima Kadi-Hanifi moved to Newman University in February 2017, where she is Senior Lecturer in Education and Multi-Professional Practice. Prior to that, she worked at the University of Worcester for nearly ten years. She led partnerships across further and higher education for Initial Teacher Training, and taught and supervised undergraduate and postgraduate students in areas as diverse as linguistics, inclusion, postgraduate research methods, English as an Additional Language (EAL), English to Speakers of Other Languages (ESOL) and Adult Literacy. She studied Linguistics at Sheffield University, obtaining a PhD in 1989, and worked first at Sheffield, followed by University College London, then Roehampton University, before settling in the West Midlands in 2007. Karima has also taught and led provision in further and in adult education both in London and in Birmingham. Her research has included sociolinguistics and speech science in the early days of her doctoral and post-doctoral career, and more recently HE learning and teaching. She has also co-authored (with Sean Bracken and Catharine Driver) a book on EAL in secondary schools, titled *Teaching English as an Additional Language in Secondary Schools: Theory and Practice* (Routledge, 2017), bringing her passion for linguistics and EAL in line with her interest in teacher education.

Carla Solvason is Senior Lecturer at the Centre for Children and Families, University of Worcester. She is the Pathway Lead for the Master's in Early Childhood and is a PhD supervisor. Along with her colleague, Rosie Walker, she co-authored *Success with Your Early Years Research Project* (Sage, 2014), which has received very positive reviews and is now a key text. Carla's first role was as a primary school teacher. During that time, she completed a Master's degree in Gender, Literature and Modernity and a PhD in Education, specifically looking at concepts of inclusion. In 2009, before starting work at Worcester, she spent a year as a consultant for the children's communication charity I CAN, and still delivers Continuing Professional Development (CPD) in speech, language and communication support.

Acknowledgements

We would like to acknowledge with thanks:

Professor Michael Crossley, University of Bristol, who is the author of *Planning and Writing a Dissertation: Working with your Adviser*, a widely used writing guide that forms the basis of Chapter 7 in this book.

Charlotte Taylor for her creative and artistic illustrations.

Sam Elliott and Rory Job for proofreading early drafts.

Imran Mohammed and Paula McElearney for their insightful suggestions on writing a postgraduate dissertation or thesis.

Carl Evans, Tien Nguyen, Ian Scott and Mark Richardson for their research on the particular learning and support needs of international students.

Professor David Green for bringing to our attention the book by L. Susan Stebbing called *Thinking to Some Purpose* (1939).

Our students for sharing with us things that they wished they had been told about academic study.

The University of Worcester for providing research and study leave to all three authors of this book.

Newman University for providing research and study leave to Karima Kadi-Hanifi halfway through the project.

Marianne Lagrange, Senior Publisher at Sage, for her support, encouragement and faith in the project as it edged towards approval.

Catriona McMullen, Jude Bowen and Robert Patterson of the editorial team at Sage for assistance in realising the finished work.

The late Gwenda Scriven for her powerful teaching sessions and materials on ethics and developing high-level research questions ('forest-to-leaf') to Foundation Degree and Master's students at the University of Worcester.

The late Dr Valerie Hall, University of Bristol, whose academic work on resilient students alerted us to the importance of survival strategies.

The late Dr Mike Atherton, University of Worcester, whose student study handout has been an inspiration.

Introduction

In this book, you will find a great deal of practical advice, help and guidance to assist you to succeed in your postgraduate (PG) studies. You may be studying a taught Master's course or Postgraduate Diploma or Certificate, or you may be following a programme leading to a research degree. We uncover the issues that are very seldom dealt with in the research literature, whether it is to do with getting along with tutors and supervisors, deciding whether you need extra emotional or academic support, or lifting your writing to the next level.

We start with you as a person, encouraging and supporting you to become mindful, reflective and more confident, aware of surroundings and opportunities, and able to negotiate the demands of academic work whilst combining this with a hectic lifestyle. Many students starting a higher degree have been out of education for several years, and therefore lack confidence and perhaps do not see themselves as academic or a high-flyer. You may be a working mum returning to study after a break, or a mature student seeking to advance in a chosen career path, or a part-time research student with a full-time job and a family. Lots of our own students are like this, and we have tried to share our joint experience to help them make the transition into postgraduate study as smooth and enjoyable as it can be.

The book is particularly targeted at students who may be less confident in their reading, writing, listening and presentation skills. Using real-life examples, we show you how to eliminate routine errors and clumsy presentation and equip you to produce work that is engaged and engaging. As well as providing some practical tips that will enable you to gain the most from your postgraduate study experience, the eight chapters in this book give helpful and accessible suggestions on how to build a persuasive argument, how to support an argument with evidence, and where to go for reliable and convincing sources, and supply you with a step-by-step guide to constructing first-class written work and presentations.

This is the first guide written specifically for those returning to education to study at postgraduate level, or who need some extra support in getting written work right. Its style is friendly, clear and authoritative, and sometimes humorous, and is written by experienced tutors in higher education (HE), who guide you through the steps needed to create highly readable, competent and confident work.

1

Understanding Yourself as a Learner and Postgraduate Student

Chapter overview

In this book, we will emphasise very strongly how much personal investment is involved in deciding to study for a higher degree and then all the choices and decisions that flow from that. So, it makes sense for us to spend some time at the outset, in this opening chapter, positioning this advanced higher education that you will embark upon around you, the postgraduate student. In this chapter, and in the book as a whole, we explicitly place you, the learner, at the centre, because we understand how important it is that your choices about university, course and approach to study are right for you. We go into this in some detail in Chapter 2 (see especially the first four sections). For ease of use, throughout the book, we use 'university' to describe all providers of higher education.

This chapter develops the idea of the postgraduate student as first and foremost a person, an individual, and recognises that all people have different needs, based upon their cultural and educational backgrounds. You will not necessarily have been a model student, and it may even be that you have struggled with some aspects of undergraduate study and the university experience more widely. You may have chosen your first university or course unwisely and are now seeking to put things right by securing an advanced university qualification, quite possibly closely connected to your current or future career. In this chapter, we try to help you understand some really important aspects of your make-up as a person that will help you to successfully negotiate this new opportunity. We offer advice on how to structure your thinking, including how to view past and present failures positively, and we suggest some tools, including meditation and mindfulness, to help you become open to study and to progressing as a person with promise. But rest assured, our approach is practical rather than mystical, and we draw on a number of different traditions and perspectives as well as on our own experience about what is helpful for postgraduate students.

Imposter syndrome

Imposter syndrome describes the feeling that, one day, sometime soon, maybe in a second or two, we are going to be caught out and exposed for the fraud that we believe that we are. All our knowledge, expertise and esteem will crumble in a moment and we will be left naked and vulnerable. It is a very common thing, and that is why it is termed a syndrome. It is especially common in universities, because the more we know, the more we are aware that we do not know. It has to do with the deepest insecurities that we all have about who we are, how we became, how others see us. And every postgraduate student will at some point, sooner or later, develop it – most likely sooner (Student Example 1.1).

Student example 1.1   Imposter syndrome: Fears without foundation

Peter is in the first term of a taught Master's in Public Administration. The first piece of assessment involves a group presentation on an organisation that has had to go through multiple changes. Peter's group persuades him to be the lead presenter as he is the most experienced. The group is well prepared and have worked up a good case study of a local authority department that has merged with another. Peter played a key part in securing one such merger in his previous work role.

As he prepares his PowerPoint, Peter becomes racked with self-doubt. He is considerably older than the others in his group, and indeed than most of the class. He worries that he will not be able to put together a coherent presentation even though he has done similar tasks many times before. He begins to think about outstanding presentations he has seen others do and is fearful that he will underperform. He starts to doubt that he is really suitable for the course and wonders why he was accepted, even though he achieved a good honours degree and a distinction for his undergraduate dissertation. He knows that the other students in the class will ask searching questions after the presentation and also knows that he will be unable to answer convincingly. He begins to accept full responsibility for the car crash that is about to happen in the classroom. All of this is a product of Peter's anxiety and worry; his fears are without foundation but that does not ease his stress. He gets through the presentation well but knows that he will be caught out next time.

Forewarned is forearmed, and knowing that imposter syndrome will inevitably strike demands that we pay some attention to the phenomenon and offer our advice on how to deal with it.

The first step in dealing with imposter syndrome is to understand that it affects everyone who interacts with others socially and professionally, so that means all of us. It has nothing to do with how qualified or experienced we are, nor has it anything to do with any weaknesses or frailties we might have. It is simply part of the human condition, in the same way as being happy or being afraid is. Imposter syndrome can be seen as an emotional condition that is generated by being in a stressful situation and perhaps being short on confidence or security at that moment. The way through it is to reflect on positives and set aside negative and disabling thoughts that lead you to question how well you can do in a class, tutorial, assignment or presentation. Focus on the desired outcome, and in particular, as a postgraduate student, get to know really well the learning outcomes of your modules and start to map your own abilities, knowledge, skills and strengths against each one. What you will then be able to do is build an armoury of positives based on your character and achievements. It is your mind that is calling into question your ability to succeed, therefore we have to control the mind and its thoughts by reflecting on our fund of strengths. We say more about how to do this further on in this chapter, in the section on 'The Observing Self'.

Personal, physical and emotional needs

It is particularly important when embarking on a new phase in life to take stock of personal, physical and emotional needs. This is very much the case when starting out on a postgraduate course. Unlike first degree courses, postgraduate courses require you to rely far more on your own resources and be more self-directed. If you are not a natural self-starter, do not worry, as there are techniques we will share with you in this book to help you on the way. There is likely to be much that is strange to you when you begin your programme: the city, the university, the course, the accommodation, the people, some or all of these will be new and unfamiliar. Although it is an exciting time, it can also be a little scary.

We strongly recommend that you make yourself familiar with the variety of student services that universities make available to all students. Most universities now organise their student services via a single portal which offers access to experienced and sympathetic staff who can offer impartial information, advice and guidance on a range of issues, including accommodation, finance and health. Often, there will be a 24-hour helpline exclusively for student use; sometimes, this service is offered by the Students' Union.

If you have relocated for your studies, it is important to register with a doctor whilst at university. This will not only be helpful in terms of treatment if you become ill during your course, but will also be helpful if an illness leads to you missing a work hand-in deadline. University mitigating circumstances procedures require you to provide evidence of the illness, and the doctor can provide a medical certificate for you.

Staying as well as you can whilst studying is really important. If you can, take regular exercise, eat wholesome foods and keep well hydrated. Exercise does not have to be done in an expensive sports facility, although most universities provide gym membership at a reasonable cost. Good alternatives are walking, cycling and swimming and there is much evidence that doing any form of regular physical exercise improves brain function. Eating well can be achieved on a modest budget, by using discount supermarkets, street markets and going for special offer lines, whilst avoiding too much in the way of processed foods, ready meals and takeaways.

Getting regular sleep is really important in enabling the body and mind to work at peak levels. Good relaxation and meditation routines are available online, or, even better, there are some excellent classes and workshops where you can learn the practices with others and under the guidance of an expert teacher. It is also good to find a 'space' to focus upon your work. If you are living with your family, it can be difficult to set aside a room for study, and whilst ideal, it is not essential. It can also be difficult if you are living in a bedsit or a campus study bedroom to separate living and working areas, but many people find it very helpful to do this wherever possible. A quiet, calm and relaxing environment is conducive to good relaxation and sleep, and is worth the effort to achieve. Oil burners, subdued lighting, comfy throws and cushions are good and inexpensive ways to help you get settled and also sleep.

Cultural influences – home and international students

One of the biggest challenges we see for international students who come to the UK to study for a postgraduate course is orientation. This involves getting up to speed very quickly with a strange physical environment, traditions and practices. In Master's- and doctoral-level study, greater independence is expected. Although there is often good student support in place, it may be different from or less obviously accessible than what is assumed to be the norm. Pedagogical practices may be very different from those previously experienced; as may tutors' demands and expectations, which may place a greater onus on the student to generate ideas, find resources and organise their time. However, these challenges can equally apply to home students who perhaps move from a rural to urban setting for the first time to study, or from an older, more traditional university to a newer one, or even in moving from one part of the country to another. Whatever the context, the best advice is to prepare thoroughly for the experience to come and, if at all possible, to have some time to spend orienting yourself to the new environment before the course begins.

A well-trodden route to a UK university for international students is the British Council, which offers excellent advice for international students on universities and courses that might meet their particular needs. Many universities have become acutely aware of the needs of international students, and have put in place opportunities and arrangements to help. In particular, it will be helpful to begin to establish strong social networks with others on the course, and, if possible, to make the time and effort to spend time with both home and international students. There may well be an International Society to join, where students can mix easily with others, perhaps from similar backgrounds and cultures. Some universities have very large numbers of international postgraduate students, and it is worth checking before applying if you know that you will be more comfortable in a more culturally diverse setting. Almost all universities have an established International Office, which organises advice services, social activities and befriending opportunities for new international students. In the next chapter, we give detailed advice on choosing a university and choosing a course (see the sections in Chapter 2, titled 'Making an Application', 'Is This the Right Course for You?' and 'Enjoying University').

Different ways of learning

Crucial to our main idea that you are at the centre of the postgraduate student experience is the recognition that each person has their own **way of learning**. Talking with friends about their course will demonstrate this: some enjoy working in the library, others hate it; some study with music in the background, others need silence; some make notes, some highlight text in books and articles, some use record cards for key ideas; some have sophisticated computer filing systems, others none. And so on. Up to a point, it is a matter of each to their own. We give some advice on organising your study in Chapter 3. Here, though, we want to lay out what is known about how students learn so that you can more easily recognise what kind of learner you are and therefore which ways of learning will work best for you (see Student Example 1.2).

Student example 1.2   Two contrasts: Outgoing and reserved

Nisha is confident and outgoing, makes friends easily, seems to have lots of them and prefers to socialise in bars, coffee shops and clubs. She is bright and articulate and learns best in a group where she can discuss ideas, try out different scenarios and think on her feet. Sai, on the other hand, is quiet and reserved, has one or two close friends but generally keeps himself to himself. He enjoys studying alone in a peaceful space and can find the library distracting when full of other students. Nisha and Sai are put together in class to prepare a presentation on international banking challenges post-Brexit. Sai spends hours researching the topic in the library and gathering articles and charts together. Nisha sets up a couple of interviews with a finance professor and a bank investment manager. They get an A grade for their project, which combines in-depth academic research with contemporary examples and commentary.

This example makes two main points. First, there are different personality types (not just the two described above, there are many more), and these affect what kind of learner you are. Second, different personalities and different learning styles can work together, because every successful group needs a range of different aptitudes and skill sets and these are never all found in the same person. A further learning point from this example is that you need to discover, if you do not realise it already, what ways of living and studying work best for you. Most importantly, never try and adopt a method that is not suitable for you. Go with what works, and create a strength out of your own character traits. However, this does not mean that you have to remain the same person forever. It is quite possible to change, but the desire to be different has to come from within and has to drive the direction of the shift rather than be led from the outside. In other words, it is no good trying to be like others if you are not and have no desire to be. On the other hand, if you are naturally quite shy and would like to be more gregarious, then the way forward might be to work on confidence-building. Take some small steps in becoming more social, perhaps try a suggestion or two with a friend or fellow student. Next in this chapter, we are going to focus on some ideas that can really help with confidence and self-expression.

Scaffolding and mind maps

For many students, organising information and ideas is quite a challenge, and it is quite possible to do this successfully as an undergraduate without ever really mastering it. As a postgraduate student, however, you are expected to work at a higher level. What does this mean? If you look at the assessment criteria for your modules and the assignments that are set by the tutors, you will find that certain words and phrases keep coming up. Typically, you are expected to be a critical reader and writer, and we go into this in some detail later in Chapters 4, 5 and 6. For now, though, we can simply say that, as postgraduates, you should be trying to connect thoughts and ideas with one another and with the existing knowledge in your field. This is different from listing. Lists show that you have mastered the content but they do not show that you can apply ideas, weigh up evidence or argue compellingly. These skills are higher-level skills and they can be learnt with a little time and application.

A good place to begin is by using **scaffolding** and **mind maps**. Scaffolding simply means building one idea onto another, developing a framework for an argument and filling this out with evidence, balancing one view against another and making suggestions or propositions based on the available evidence. Much like a builder uses scaffolding to construct a building, one piece at a time, some going vertically, some horizontally, some at an angle. It is a very good metaphor for how you will need to build thoughts and ideas into a structured argument for an essay, presentation or assignment. At the most advanced levels of postgraduate study, you will contribute originality of thought by applying existing ideas and theories in new and different contexts, or even by developing new ideas and theory. But, at all levels of postgraduate study, the ability to connect is key. Keep the scaffold in mind for every piece of work.

There are many kinds of mind maps that can help in organising your ideas and sources in preparation for writing. The simplest is in the form of a tree, with the trunk as the main topic, the large branches as sub-topics or themes that you will cover, and smaller branches and offshoots as the different points that you will cover to develop your argument (see Drawing 1.1 and Student Example 1.3).

Student example 1.3   A tree mind map

Jess has to plan a sports industry management assignment on the impact of digitisation in a sport of her choice. She is a national women's football player so she chooses football. She understands that the topic will apply quite broadly across the sport so she needs to focus and channel her ideas into a specific number of themes, in which she can develop an argument about the strong impact that digital technology and software has had. She begins a mind map showing on the trunk the main topic, and on the large branches the key themes that the assignment will cover. The smaller branches pick up the various points that she initially decides will help to make her argument compelling. The mind map is incomplete, and she will add to it and extend is as she does more

(Continued)

research on the subject. A couple of the larger branches are empty. This is to remind her to stay open to the possibility of further key themes arising from her research, which can be added later. However, she is careful to set herself a deadline to complete the tree so as to avoid indefinitely adding to the field of topics and never completing the task (procrastination).

DRAWING 1.1   Tree

Resilience and perseverance

One of the most striking attributes of postgraduate students is their **resilience and perseverance**. Often, students commit to studying and completing a postgraduate course against incredible odds, combining study and raising a family, working full-time or in one or more part-time jobs, and the many other demands and pressures of day-to-day living. We show in the next chapter how paid work and study can be effectively combined to earn as you learn through work-based learning (WBL) approaches. However, it remains the case that for most students, coursework has to be managed alongside a plethora of other demands and commitments, and this requires enormous mental strength and determination. Help is available, for example from tutors and student services, if the pressures become too great. And all of us struggle at some time or other with juggling our work and personal life. This does not claim to be a self-help book explaining techniques for mind over matter; however, we can share our experiences as to what approaches have helped many other students, and also help you to avoid some of the common pitfalls.

Postgraduate study certainly makes heavy demands on students. There are lectures, seminars or tutorials to attend, pre-reading to be done for each of those, and, of course, the inevitable deadlines that must be met. The key point that we want to make in this section is that resilience and perseverance are attitudes of mind, dispositions that can be learnt and developed. The starting point is to think positively about the demands that will be made in the course, and plan ahead. As the saying goes, 'failing to plan is planning to fail'. Assessment criteria are included with each module guide. Only if you study these carefully will you understand exactly what you need to do to pass and to achieve higher grades. Assignment deadlines are published well in advance, so you can make a calendar of deadlines. We suggest that instead of seeing deadlines as a series of giant hurdles to be leaped over, you regard deadlines as an opportunity to structure your learning, to organise your work, and to plan ahead how you will occupy your days and weeks. Resilient learners have strategies to achieve their goals, and learn to adapt and be flexible when life events get in the way of well-made plans (Student Example 1.4).

Student example 1.4   Plan for these

Ayo is studying for a Postgraduate Certificate in Urban Geography. He is taking a module on Community Participation in Urban Strategies, alongside four other modules. He studies the module assignment deadlines for all his modules and notes that, unfortunately, three of his modules have assignment deadlines that are very close together,

(Continued)

immediately after the Christmas and New Year break. It is November, and Ayo plans to go back to Ghana for the upcoming holiday. He decides to sort out his work so that he can complete the planning and preparation for one assignment – a presentation that has to be made in the first week after his return in the New Year – before he leaves for Ghana.

He explains his thinking and problem to the group, and they agree that it would be good to go with Ayo's plan, as they all have similarly bunched assignment deadlines. This is a busy time of the year for the students. They work together and assign group roles, spreading the workload as evenly and fairly as they can. When they break up for the holidays, they feel well prepared for the class presentation to come in January. Ayo also has two essays due in the first week back. He knows that he needs a lot of time to plan for these and to do the reading. He knows that he needs to avoid asking for extensions as these simply pile on more pressure, overlapping with the next round of assignment deadlines.

He books his flight to Accra four days after the end of term. The library will be open 24/7 and he will plan to work flat-out to finish one essay before he goes home. That leaves one essay to be done on his return. He will take some articles to Ghana but knows that he will probably not look at them. This does not matter as he will have time on his return to focus on the remaining essay and comfortably meet the hand-in date.

Group work, in particular, demands planning and attention to when, where and how tasks will be completed. Setting milestones for each phase or aspect of a project will help to ensure that the work progresses smoothly and that each person's role is specified. Building some contingency time or 'slack' into the schedule will help to overcome any unforeseen delays,complications, or even the more pleasurable problem of holidays.

The observing self (meditation and mindfulness)

There are numerous books and videos available on developing the skills and habits of meditation and mindfulness. It is not necessary to go entirely with a spiritual approach to life in order to experience the benefits of developing an observing self. What we mean by this is 'reflexivity': the ability to think positively and with a broad awareness of yourself in your own situation, your life as you live it. Reflecting on your strengths and past achievements, and understanding that you have the power within you to do well and to achieve the goals you set yourself. Also, part of this is to understand that the mind will often lead you towards self-doubt, undermining your confidence, sometimes bringing you to doubt that you will ever be able to make it to the end.

We believe that it is really important to realise that as a student you will meet hundreds of challenges, large and small, and that your mindset can play a critical part in shaping the outcome. The observing self understands that keeping the medium-term objectives (e.g., attending classes, handing in assignments on time) and long-term objectives (e.g., passing the course, getting a graduate job) in view goes a long way towards maintaining positive influences on the mind.

There are many classes and courses on meditation and mindfulness available online and as apps such as Headspace, Calm, The Mindfulness App and Smiling Mind. All of these can be helpful in guiding you towards effective techniques for decluttering your mind and focusing on the here and now. A relaxed, open and prepared mind is more conducive to positive and productive approaches in general, and will certainly help you to deal effectively with the ups and downs of student life.

It is perfectly possible to develop these techniques by yourself, but many people find it helpful to learn the practice of meditation and mindfulness under the guidance of a teacher and with others in a group. Many universities have such groups that meet regularly, and these can be a good discipline in providing a regular time and space to focus your thoughts and energies on improvement and personal progress.

Key ideas and terms

Imposter syndrome describes the feeling that, one day, sometime soon, maybe today, we are going to be caught out and exposed for the fraud that we suppose we are. It affects almost everyone, is unrelated to how qualified and experienced we are, and can be managed through positive thinking.

Cultural influences are without doubt a tremendously positive aspect of the UK higher education scene. They can at the same time bring about feelings of otherness and alienation that can be upsetting and stressful. Successful integration requires some organisation and participation, as well as preparation in choosing as far as possible an environment where you will feel comfortable.

Ways of learning are sometimes known as 'learning styles', and reflect very real differences between people in terms of personality and disposition. This can apply to whether you learn best individually or in groups, whether you prefer practical or theoretical approaches, or whether you prefer somewhere quiet where you can focus or more noisy, social learning spaces. It is most important to understand how you learn and to let this influence your course choice and to plan your learning environment around this.

Scaffolding simply means building one idea onto another, building a framework for an argument and filling this out with evidence, balancing one view against another and making suggestions or propositions based on the available evidence.

Mind maps come in many forms, and can help in organising your ideas and sources in preparation for writing. The simplest is in the form of a tree, with the trunk as the main topic, the large branches as sub-topics or themes that you will cover, and the smaller branches and offshoots as the different points that you will cover in order to develop your argument.

Resilience and perseverance are common traits in those who combine studying with working and come to the fore when coursework has to be managed alongside a plethora of other demands and commitments, and this requires enormous mental strength and determination. Help is available if the pressures become too great. And all of us struggle at some time or other with juggling our work and personal life. Resilient learners have strategies to achieve their goals, and learn to adapt and be flexible when life events get in the way of well-made plans.

The observing self (meditation and mindfulness). What we mean by this is reflexivity: the ability to think positively and with a broad awareness of yourself in your own situation, and your life as you live it. Reflecting on your strengths and past achievements, and understanding that you have the power within you to do well and achieve the goals you set yourself.

Chapter summary

The focus of this chapter is on placing you, the student, at the centre of postgraduate study. We emphasise the importance of taking control of your study through planning and preparation. At the same time, we recognise that we all occasionally suffer from imposter syndrome, and we explain what that is and how to deal with it as a natural and normal consequence of almost any sort of social or business engagement. Taking stock of personal, physical and emotional needs is another aspect of maintaining control, and we highlight the support services widely available for students, and show how some simple self-help techniques can shape the mind towards a positive outlook. We recognise that some students face a significant social and cultural shift when embarking on postgraduate study and we offer advice to help in orientation and integration. The chapter ends with a recognition that, although we all have our own particular way of learning and need to devise strategies that suit us best, there are some well-tried and tested ways of organising and assimilating information that can greatly help in making effective use of the study time available.

2

The Study Environment

Chapter overview

This chapter explores the process of **applying to university**, studying there, and the support that will be available for you. We try and demystify this process, and we encourage you to be confident about making your choices and planning your studies. In particular, we recognise that many postgraduate students have to balance postgraduate study with other demands, including home, family, partner and job. For this reason, we have tried to structure our advice and guidance so that it is clear, realistic and applicable across a variety of different contexts. For example, the section on 'Earn as You Learn' recognises that most postgraduates will need to work and study, whether they are on a part-time or full-time course.

However, we believe that this combination of work and study can be positive. Obviously, the main purpose of anyone working is the wage, but work can also be a good release from the pressures of academic study, and, sometimes, for example through modules that have a focus on students' own work experiences or work-based learning, it can provide a context and even a focus for coursework and projects. The section on 'Using the Library' may contain little that is new for some readers. However, our experience is that some students fail to make the most of the resources available. We hope that the chapter will encourage those who may be a little fearful about embarking on postgraduate study. We are confident that, should you follow our advice, you will do well and succeed.

Making an application

Applying for a postgraduate course is quite similar to applying for a job. For postgraduate study in the UK, there is no central clearing process like UCAS.

You apply for the course or courses you want to do and complete the university's application form, often found on their website. In the UK Framework of Higher Education Qualifications, Master's and Postgraduate Certificate Courses are categorised as Level 7, whilst doctorates of all kinds are at Level 8. These Levels are a system of classification for HE, beginning with Levels 4, 5 and 6, which in the case of a three-year full-time honours degree denote the increasing learning challenge in years 1, 2 and 3. In all cases, you simply find the course or programme that attracts you, and make your application.

This section is mainly about what things we, as course tutors, are looking for in an application. Most university courses select students for postgraduate courses on the merits of the written application form alone. The exception is for professional courses, which almost always require an interview.

Postgraduate courses vary greatly in popularity, the same as undergraduate courses. There are, therefore, some postgraduate courses that are highly selective and, once you have chosen the course you want to do, a strong and powerful application is really a must. Here, we focus on the personal statement that is part of the majority of application forms. It is here that you will need to convince the admissions tutor or potential supervisor that they should select you above other candidates. The application statement is your first opportunity to demonstrate that you understand how to convey ideas in an academic voice, that you can show originality and spark, and that you can express yourself with focus and clarity.

There are four areas of life (we look at each one in turn below) that you will need to connect in your personal statement: your personal experience; the course you have applied for; the wider university; and the relevant employment sector that you hope the course will lead to. We will think about this as your story. It is a personal story, because it begins with you, and as we keep emphasising, *you* are the most important element at the centre of this whole process.

So, what elements of your personal biography are relevant? If you are applying for an early years course, you will want to say something about your experience and values as a parent or carer perhaps, and if you have professional experience in the area, then that, too. If you are applying for a media course, what were the early influences on your interests, which genres have attracted you and why? How have you been able to follow these interests as an undergraduate and where do you want to take them at postgraduate level? To repeat, this is your story, and the tutors will be looking for how central the course is going to be to you as a person and what you will bring, from your skills and experience, to the course.

Now for the course or programme itself. Tutors like you to know what it is that you are actually applying for, so, you will need to do a bit of work finding out about the course, what broad areas it covers, the balance of theory and practice, and where it can lead to in terms of employment and employability. What two or three modules look particularly interesting, and why? Can you link any of these to your undergraduate interests, and especially what elements of your independent study or final project can you draw from and build on at postgraduate level? If you are going straight into university at Master's level from industry, you will need to make the connections between the course and your current or past employment. If you are going for a professional course, this should be straightforward, but the tutors will be looking for you to make specific connections, say between a particular interest that you have and one or more course modules, rather than just generic and unsupported statements like: 'I am interested in...' They will be looking for you to make the connections, for these to be specific and detailed and considered, and, again, for the link between the course and you, the person. You need to make it real and avoid enthusing without concrete examples of where elements of the course will open up avenues for you, make connections with your past study or employment, and perhaps pick out one or two aspects that you find particularly interesting and where you might want to specialise. If there is a possibility that you might progress to do postgraduate research, say this, and, again, indicate which aspects might attract you to delve deeper.

You will, of course, be able to participate more widely in the life of the university that you choose than just attending modules. Tutors will appreciate it if you have some knowledge of, and interest in, the wider opportunities available at the university. These might include volunteering in an area related to the course. Some law courses, for example, enable students to practice in an advisory capacity for local residents facing legal issues. The university will have drama groups, choirs, sports teams and perhaps a student radio station. Most universities organise volunteering, often through the Students' Union, across a range of sectors, which can provide valuable personal and professional development opportunities as well as a chance to connect with and contribute something to the local community.

If you are a research student, you may have an opportunity to contribute to teaching in your department, thus gaining valuable experience of working in higher education. Full-time Master of Research (MRes) and Doctor of Philosophy (PhD, DPhil) students who gain a studentship may well have some course-teaching and even administration duties included as a mandatory part of their contract. Although this can be a good opportunity for work experience, care should be taken that the required hours of work are proportionate and do not exceed the contracted maximum.

Employability is a key aim of all postgraduate courses, not just the professional ones. You will be able to find out about the standard employment outcomes for students who graduate from your chosen course. And, by consulting the Unistats data set available online for every UK university course, you will be able to discover what the programme designers believe that the course will provide in terms of employability skills, career enhancement and attributes. Your personal statement should make it very clear that you appreciate and understand what the course will do to enhance your employ-ability, and if you have a long-term career ambition that the course will support, then make clear your aims.

All this work on the personal statement will not be wasted. You can tailor and adapt the statement for other course applications and for job applica-tions, too. But, crucially, the process of thinking about your story and why and how the programme fits into it will help you decide if the course is really right for you.

Is this the right course for you?

Choosing a course at postgraduate level can be more straightforward than choosing one when going to university for the first time as an under-graduate. If you are a recent graduate, you will be aware of courses offered by your own university and especially in your department. Some universities and colleges offer fee discounts to graduates who progress onto postgraduate courses in the same institution. If you are set on a career in one of the profes-sions, there are courses tailored for you, such as the Postgraduate Certificate in Education (PGCE), which confer qualified teacher status. These are termed 'professional courses' and you will be familiar with others, in health and law for example.

However, if you graduated some time ago, or you are coming to Master's level study as a student for the first time based on your industrial or profes-sional experience, your decision may be more complicated because there are hundreds of universities and other providers of postgraduate courses to choose from. This number is set to grow as the government makes it easier for new providers to enter the higher education market, and postgraduate loans are widely available.

If you are not looking for a postgraduate course linked to a specific profes-sion, your choice is even wider. There are specialist taught postgraduate courses in an enormous variety of subjects spanning the whole array of Arts, Humanities, Sciences and Professional Studies. Many of these are available to both full-time and part-time students. Master's study can be a form of Continuing Professional Development (CPD), with some students doing as little as one Master's module a year. Credits can be transferred to and from other universities as there is one National Qualifications Framework (NQF) for higher education. This introduces a further level of decision-making, and there is no single Pocket Book of Answers. It is not simply a matter of whether you will need to work or not whilst you study. Most postgraduate students work alongside studying, except perhaps the small minority fortunate enough to have been able to secure a studentship or grant. Clearly, this is easier to do as a part-time postgraduate student than as a full-time student, since the workload will be more manageable. We say more about this in the section on 'Earn as You Learn'.

Most people choose their postgraduate course because they like the sound of the course itself, or because it will enable them to achieve a professional qualification to enter or enhance their chosen career, rather than because they are attracted to the university or course provider per se. However, in regions of the country where there are few educational institutions offering postgraduate courses, there is a big exception to this. In this case, the choice will be more directly linked to and limited by the universities and other providers available nearby. Many people living in isolated rural areas who are tied to that area by family, home or job cannot choose to move and so must either study locally or choose to enrol onto a postgraduate degree by distance learning. Most courses require some amount of engagement with online learning, but some are taught almost exclusively online. Those offered by the Open University are perhaps the most familiar, although most universities now offer this mode, and there is a considerable range of subjects, including professional courses, on offer. However, it is the case that not all people are comfortable with distance learning, and prefer the human interaction, peer support and teaching and learning experience of courses that require regular attendance.

DRAWING 2.1 Pocket Book of Answers

It is not our purpose to encourage you to choose one or another mode of study for your postgraduate course. All people are different, and research has shown that different people learn in different ways. Some prefer and are quite happy studying in isolation, only interacting with their tutors. Others prefer and even need fellow students to talk with, to test ideas, to share problems, to work in collaboration on projects and assignments. There is no right or wrong here: we are all different and the important thing is to know what kind of learner you are. If you have recently graduated, you will probably be fairly clear about this. Think back to the elements of those courses that you enjoyed and those that you did not. What were the key characteristics that led you to engage more with some modules than with others? How important was peer-group support in helping your progress through the course? These are really important questions, and, likely as not, choosing a course where the mode of study fits your own style will be the major determinant of how well you will do, and certainly of how much you will enjoy the experience.

One of the more readily noticeable differences between postgraduate courses is the extent to which they are 'theoretical' and 'practical'. We have used inverted commas because, of course, these are not in any way mutually exclusive characteristics. Courses can, and almost all do, involve both theory and practice. Indeed, one of the characteristics of study at postgraduate level is to be able to see how both theory and practice come together, and all the later chapters here deal with some different aspects of the theory/practice relationship.

That said, without doubt some courses place a higher emphasis on doing and creating, whilst others place more emphasis on interpretation and analysis. If you think about the different kinds of activity you might be involved in as a postgraduate student, you will undoubtedly be more attracted to some of them than to others. Think, for example, about workshops, visits, physical activities, presentations, rehearsals, shows, performances, production. Some of these will involve a high level of group work and activity. How will you respond to that? For some, a group project that fully involves and stretches all members, calling for different skills to be brought together, will be a highlight of the course. For others, it will be a source of frustration and disappointment, especially when things do not go well. It is important, then, to be clear about what your own preferences are.

How do you find out what a course will be like? Of course, there is the university prospectus, but that only gives the 'formal' academic gloss on the course. What is it really like? Good ways to find out are: talk to former students or current students on that course; visit the university and speak to staff who teach it; see what is available on social media about the course; simply visit the campus for a while and talk to as many people as possible. Once again, we want to stress that the key thing is whether the course is right for you. *You* are the most important element in deciding what course to opt for. You will have access to many forms of quality assessment, such as those offered by the Quality Assurance Agency for Higher Education (QAA), Research Excellence Framework (REF) and Teaching Excellence Framework (TEF), newspaper rankings of subjects and universities, national student surveys, destination surveys, success rates and employment rates. But all of these – important as they may be in and of themselves – are trumped by how well the course fits your tastes, your learning style. If you find the course that best suits you, then you will be energised and inspired by the experience.

Enjoying university

A quick look at different university websites will show you what aspects of university life each institute or faculty is prioritising as their unique selling points. Some universities place a strong emphasis on scholarship and research over students and teaching. Others focus on business links and employability. Many universities give a lot space to the student experience, including accommodation, students' union social activities, sports societies, volunteering opportunities, pre-sessional courses for international students and so on. City universities will highlight the benefits of urban living, whereas campus universities will emphasise the benefits of a range of facilities, all on-site. Universities are very different from each other, and therefore choosing one university over another requires some care.

As we have emphasised before, the key ingredient of a successful choice is you: What is important to you when thinking about a place where you will spend some considerable time gaining a higher degree? If your chosen course is very specialist, then this may be quite a restricted choice. However, for most students, postgraduate courses in Professional Studies, Health and Education are on offer in most universities as well as in many colleges and private providers. That said, if you have family responsibilities, a mortgage or are working in a job that you intend to stay in, geographical location is likely to be an overriding factor in choosing where to study. There may be only one or two universities within daily travelling distance that offer the course that you want to do. Each personal situation is different and we can only offer general guidance, but even if your institution choice is fairly limited, we recommend that you make a list of aspects and features that you definitely do and do not want (Student Example 2.1). In almost every case, the most appropriate course for your interests will be the strongest 'must have', and that is why we focused on this in the section above on 'Is This the Right Course for You?' However, other aspects are more about the university itself and can be critical to your student experience.

Student example 2.1   Planning for the right place, work and course

Joanna was accepted on a full-time MA in Creative Writing. As she had applied late, all the university accommodation had been taken and she was placed on a reserve list for a room. The university placed her in 'university approved' lodgings in a nearby seaside town. Although Joanna quite enjoyed being by the sea, she had no private transport, and whilst buses were convenient during the day, they did not continue to run in the evenings. Also, nearly all of the other students were on campus and so most of the social activities tended to be on campus as well. Joanna felt a bit isolated and had to pay for a taxi if she wanted to stay late for any reason.

Ranjit is a full-time PhD research student. His subject is on Social Housing and, after he graduates, he hopes to become a chartered planner and work in urban planning. The Students' Union provided dozens of volunteer opportunities, and advertised for students interested in volunteering at a housing and benefits advice service in the city centre. Ranjit applied and was successful in getting a volunteer post for three hours a week whilst he completed his programme. When he applied for an urban planner post in a large city authority department, his volunteering experience helped to convince the interview panel of his dedication and commitment and he was offered the job.

Louisa enrolled on a one-year full-time MSc in Business Finance. Just after she started the course, her partner, who is self-employed, became ill and could no longer work. Money became a problem and Louisa went to see the university Finance Officer, who arranged with the university Registry for her to amend her registration to part-time so that she could work whilst studying. Because she had enrolled on a course with full-time and part-time modes available, Louisa could continue her studies over a longer period, whilst freeing up more time for her to earn in order to ease the financial situation of herself and her partner.

These examples illustrate the need to plan as far ahead as possible, to take advantage of opportunities that university will provide to complement the academic experience, to seek appropriate advice, and to be prepared to be flexible and imaginative when difficulties arise.

In this book, we have generally used the term 'university' to describe the institution in which you study. However, there are other options available. Some further education (FE) colleges offer postgraduate courses. These are generally in specialist areas that the college has particular expertise in, with highly qualified and experienced staff to teach it, and state-of-the-art facilities. The Higher Education and Research Act 2017 includes provision for additional higher education institutions that will be able to award postgraduate degrees. An open day visit, or an arranged visit, or even a casual drop-in-and-see visit, will tell you all you need to know to make an informed decision on whether the course will be right for you.

We need to declare an interest that all three of us work in established universities. However, not least because many of the new institutions in 2017 will be 'for profit' institutions, we urge extreme care in selecting one of these. The qualifications and experience of staff, the robustness of the academic structures and governance, and any independent assessments of the quality of learning and teaching should be taken into account – not only in judging new institutions but established universities as well. The National Student Survey (NSS) provides a guide to how satisfied current third year undergraduate students are with their courses and their university, and you can perform a search by institution and by subject to find information on this, which is updated annually. Just as schools and colleges are subject to quality checks by the Office for Standards in Education (Ofsted), so, too, are higher education institutions subject to quality control by the Quality Assurance Agency for Higher Education, and their reports are published on their website. Postgraduate teacher education courses are given quality ratings by Ofsted, and professional courses in health, psychology and social work are given quality ratings by the Health and Care Professions Council. The Research Excellence Framework (REF) is a well-established government mechanism that uses peer review of research outputs to rank, and drive government funding for, university research. A Teaching Excellence Framework for higher education has been introduced as part of the Higher Education and Research Act 2017. This ranks university teaching and will be used to determine which universities can increase tuition fees.

Earn as you learn

'**Earn as you learn**' is a useful phrase that describes a fact of life for most students. Ever since student fees for undergraduates were settled at around £9000 per annum, postgraduate fees have climbed to reflect these, so that typical fees in 2017 for a UK student applying for a one-year full-time Master's course – 180 Master's (M) level Credits – or a PhD are in the region of the amounts listed in Table 2.1.

TABLE 2.1 Typical fees for a UK student applying for a one-year full-time Master's course – 180 Master's (M) level Credits – or a PhD, 2017

Course	Fees (£)
MA Childhood and Youth	5,400
MA Business and Management	6,800
MSc Psychological Research	7,216
Master of Business Administration (MBA)	8,100–35,650
MSc Healthcare Policy and Management	10,700
PhD Urban Studies and Planning	4,194

TABLE 2.2   Examples of part-time annual course fees set pro rata to the full-time fee

Part-time annual course fee	Fees set pro rata to the full-time fee (£)
Postgraduate Certificate in Primary English (Year One 30 M Level Credits)	1,380
Postgraduate Certificate in Primary English (Year One 30 M Level Credits)	1,380
Postgraduate Certificate in Teenage and Young Adult Cancer Care (60 M Level Credits)	1,671
Postgraduate Diploma in Human Resource Management (120 M Level Credits)	10,121
Postgraduate Certificate in Education (M Credits vary from 30–90 between courses)	9,000
Doctorate in Education (EdD)	3,120

As you can see, there is a fair amount of variation in postgraduate course fees. The above examples are taken at the time of writing from different universities. Note that fees for overseas students are considerably higher and can be up to three times the fee for a UK student. We have included a fee range for the MBA to show that many universities charge a significant premium for this academic award.

Part-time annual course fees are generally set pro rata to the full-time fee. Some examples are given in Table 2.2.

Some fees for courses targeted at health and education professionals are set lower to be more affordable for those paying for themselves rather than being supported by their employer or by the government (e.g., some PGCEs and some Master's courses in Social Work). Price competition is likely to become greater as more institutions become able to offer postgraduate qualifications, however the maxim *caveat emptor* (let the buyer beware) is one to bear in mind.

So, we have established that getting a Master's or doctorate is not cheap. Although the government has recently introduced loans for postgraduate students, this may not be such good news for those who are debt averse and who may already have incurred £60,000 or more of debt to acquire a first degree. In this section, then, we want to show that to earn as you learn is a viable and realistic ambition and that it is quite possible to work and study at the same time, and we want to reassure you that many students have done so very successfully without jeopardising their academic study and prospects.

It may be that 'earn as you learn' is at the heart of your strategy for postgraduate study (Student Example 2.2).

Student example 2.2   Work and study

Mahdi has a degree in Theatre Studies and Media Production and gained a good job working in media sales for a national newspaper. He wants to study for a Master's but his financial circumstances and personal preference mean that he wants to do this part-time, over two or three years. He enrols on an MBA course at his local university. He has in mind to start his own company some day, using his knowledge and experience at the newspaper to branch out on his own. The course that he has chosen is strongly **work-based**. So, Mahdi can use his knowledge skills gained in his day-to-day job as a resource for the assignments towards the credits that he will need to accumulate. Most of the modules on his course require the student to link business and management theory to practical situations, and so Mahdi can easily identify work-based problems in his office and in the wider company on which to base his assignments. The course also requires him to submit a dissertation worth 45 credits, which is a quarter of the credits needed for his course. This will be on different models of media sales, and will eventually be valuable research for his next challenge of starting his own business.

Having accepted that working whilst studying is an inescapable reality for most postgraduate students, it is clearly far preferable if the paid work can complement the study, as in Student Example 2.2. However, as well as contributing to meeting the cost of study, any paid work can be valuable additional experience. Work can, in itself, be a useful outlet when the pressures of study grow, and the friendships made with colleagues can be a valuable source of support. Also, increasingly employers look for evidence of employability when appointing graduates, and periods spent in part-time work whilst studying can evidence your motivation to succeed and a track record of reliability. The additional employability skills arising through your study are considered in Chapter 8. Perhaps a word of warning, though, that paid work can be a distraction and, in itself, a source of anxiety and stress. An ideal scenario is that the work is flexible, fulfilling, reasonably paid but not too strenuous. Each person is different, so experience is a valuable guide as to what works best for you. It should help to know that many students manage to earn while they learn and to achieve a good work/life/study balance.

Using the library

The starting point for completing the tasks and assignments that you need to pass in order to achieve the degree is the module resource list that will be published alongside other details for every module that comprises your course. Module **resource lists** vary enormously from tutor to tutor. Some are extremely lengthy, with essential and recommended reading, and a variety of book, journal and internet sources, whilst others will be more focused. Module tutors are required to keep resource lists up to date, and will ensure that the literature included in them is central to the theme and topics of the module, and is current and accessible. These lists are deposited at **the university library**, which ensures that the specialist subject librarian is familiar with the reading that is being recommended to students, and that the library has a good range of the printed and electronic material in stock.

Some of the core and most popular books listed as required reading will often be available only on short-term loan. This is done in order that as many students as possible can gain access to these items. Others may be designated as reference only, and so cannot be taken out of the library. Clearly, then, in the case of books that are designated as essential and recommended reading, due to popular demand, there may be difficulties in accessing these as and when you would like them. Some tutors ensure that core texts are available from the university bookshop or the local academic bookshop, so that purchasing the item(s) may be an option for some students. Often, where a core text is used year after year on a module, students sell these on cheaply to new students via notice board adverts. However, increasingly core reading material for modules is made available electronically through the library systems so that all students are able to access it.

There are many benefits to the postgraduate student in focusing primarily on journal articles as the key source of theoretical literature for each module. Their quality is assured because of the rigorous process of peer review. Generally, between 5000 and 8000 words in length, and focused on a specific topic, they can be a succinct, reliable and easily accessible source of ideas and material for assignments. Articles are available via the university library Web portal via an access code, usually your university log-in ID and password. Thus, whilst these resources originate from the university library, you can access them via a PC, tablet or smart phone, print them off, and build up your own resource bank of relevant reading materials. Articles are often more up to date than books, with some journals publishing issues as frequently as once a month. Sometimes, articles prompt other articles that challenge or complement issues raised in the original. Your library may well still hold print copies of journals in your field, and these can be useful for browsing and getting an overview of a field, especially if you are new to it. However, increasingly, libraries subscribe to electronic copies only, so any browsing must be done online. See the section in Chapter 4 on 'Accessing Literature Online' for more information on this.

Although increasingly much of the theoretical literature used for research is accessed online, libraries remain inspiring spaces in which to work. We recommend allotting some time each week if possible, to spend in the university library, browsing, consulting with the university subject librarian, reading and writing. Libraries are generally most conducive to study, and it can be very helpful to get into the habit of going, because it will help to foster the good habit of reading and writing. Most universities have extended opening hours compared with public libraries, so you can choose the most convenient time for you to designate as your own library space. The Society of College, National and University Libraries (SCONUL) scheme enables students to access university libraries nearer their home or workplace.

Key ideas and terms

Applying to university will involve an application form accompanied by a personal statement that will need to connect four areas of life – yourself, the course you have applied for, the wider university, and the relevant employment sector that you hope the course will lead to – that will persuade the Admissions Tutor that you are a suitable candidate.

Choosing a postgraduate course will require you to consider elements of your degree that you enjoyed and those that you did not, whether you prefer classes or distance learning, whether you enjoy practical or theoretical work.

There is a lot of information available to help you make the right decision, including quality assessments, newspaper rankings of subjects and universities, national student surveys, destination surveys, success rates and employment rates. All of these are important but the key thing is whether the course is right for you: how well the course fits your tastes; your learning style; how far you, as a person, will be energised and inspired by the experience.

More universities and other kinds of HE providers are being created to encourage competition and a market in higher education, which may well mean that some institutions provide more of a 'no-frills', cheaper, albeit more basic, student experience.

Enjoying university means different things to different people, and universities are very different in what they are good at and what facilities they provide, their links with employers and where they are located, so it is well worth spending some time visiting either at an Open Day or just turning up to have a look around.

Earn as you learn is a viable and realistic ambition. It is quite possible to work and study at the same time, and many students have done so very successfully without jeopardising their academic study and prospects.

Work-based learning (WBL) makes it possible to combine working in a profession, business or industrial setting with academic study, and many postgraduate courses are available that use WBL across much of the course content.

Resource lists are central to planning your module study as the literature included in them is central to the theme and topics of the module, and is current and accessible.

The university library can be a productive and inspirational space to work in, and even though most of its resources can be accessed online, regular visits will encourage the good habit of reading and writing.

Chapter summary

This chapter gives detailed advice on preparing an application for postgraduate study and focuses especially on the personal statement, which gives the opportunity to convince the university Admissions Tutor that you are a suitable candidate. Some key differences between universities and postgraduate courses are highlighted in order to help you make a choice. We recognise that many students have to combine paid work with study, and we show how 'earn as you learn' can be a positive way of enhancing your academic programme. We suggest that using the library is a valuable part of the student experience, and that even though most of the resources that you will need for your assignments can be accessed online, regular sessions in the library can help to foster the good habit of reading and writing.

3

The Unspoken Rules of Academic Etiquette

Chapter overview

In this chapter, we explore the idea of general guidelines for 'acceptable behaviour' during your postgraduate study. It will give you an indication of what is expected of you, but also of what you might expect of others. As a rule, approaches to academic etiquette are rarely verbalised and they are certainly not put in print, but instead they are picked up along the course of your academic journey through trial and error. Hopefully, this chapter will help to reduce your margin for error. Although interpersonal relationships will always be unique to the particular context and the individuals involved, being more informed about them will enable you to be better prepared for all eventualities. In this chapter, the main focus will be on relationships with your tutors, other university staff and your peers. But the discussion will also encompass issues of time management and the ownership of your individual study.

Contacting your tutors

As you embark on academic study at postgraduate level, a key aspect of your success is going to be the relationships that you build with your tutors. You may have a range of university tutors if you are studying taught modules, or you may have a supervisory team if you are working on individual research.

Whatever the mode of your study, the likelihood is that you will be working in smaller groups and more intimately with these tutors than you have done during your undergraduate study. The relationship will be slightly different. There is no rule of thumb for what this type of relationship will actually look like, as your tutors, like the rest of society, will come in all shapes and sizes. You will encounter tutors who are warm and open, who will offer you as much emotional as academic support, and you will have the more reserved 'teachers' who will keep a professional distance. Because of this, we are going to suggest neither an overly enthusiastic greeting nor a formal shake of the hand when you first meet your new tutors. You will need to wait to follow their lead, but what we do strongly suggest in all cases is openness and honesty.

From the outset, it should be clear what the mutual expectations of your relationship with your tutors are: if these expectations are not clear, then make sure to ask. If you are not being taught by your tutors but are only being supervised, then you are likely to establish initial contact via email or telephone. Try to arrange to meet your tutor face to face as soon as you are able, because being able to put a face to a name really improves the quality of the relationship that you have. Within your first weeks of study, the parameters should be firmly established around:

- How it is best to contact your tutor.
- How often they will expect you to contact them.
- Who should propose tutorials.
- What format these meetings will take.
- Where it is best to meet.

When you are a little further into your studies, you will also want to know about gaining feedback on your written work. You will need to have a clear understanding of what your tutors are willing to give feedback on, for example plans or drafts and whether they are willing to look at a section, a page or the complete document. You will also need to be clear about whether, once you have made changes in response to feedback, they are willing to look at the work again. If you are anxious about any aspect of your study, then let them know. They cannot help you if they do not know that there is a problem. If there is information that still confuses you, then ask them about it. The best way forward in your academic relationship is through frank and honest dialogue. You have just started a new course and no one will expect you to know all the answers. Start with the guidance found in handbooks and module outlines, but if that does not give you the answers then do not be afraid to ask.

DRAWING 3.1 Do *not* disturb

Emails

If you are a research student, it may be left to you to initiate individual contact with your tutor. The nature of postgraduate study is that the student takes the lead. Please do remember that you are not their only student, they may have dozens, if not hundreds (depending on their roles outside of postgraduate teaching), so it is always a good idea to remind them of who you are in your email correspondence. It is not unusual for tutors to regularly receive emails such as this:

Hi, can I come and see you about the assignment? Tomorrow or Friday are good for me.

Kate ☺ x

This approach to emailing is not going to be terribly helpful, for a number of reasons that are worth exploring. First, is the area of professionalism. No matter how friendly your tutor may be towards you, they are still your tutor. There should be an element of formality (and, although it seems terribly old-fashioned to say it, respect) in your written communications with them. Remember that it is not a text to a friend, but a professional enquiry to a tutor. Emails are likely to be a key aspect of your future profession and it is worth developing an appropriate tone and approach with these whilst you study. Develop yourself a 'Dear …, Yours sincerely,' template that you use for all interactions with academic staff.

The second issue that this example raises is that it is not unusual for a tutor to teach somewhere in the region of four Kates (or Clares or Gemmas …) at any one time. It is often impossible to know who this particular 'Kate' is or which module or course they belong to just from a university email address – and that is if you actually use your university email address. It becomes even more difficult when the email address in the 'Sent by' field is 'hotpants69@internetserve.com'. Please think very carefully about the impression that you are giving through your email 'name' and consider whether another account may need to be opened for your academic and professional emails. Set yourself an email signature that includes your full name, course and student number if used at postgraduate level. In the email, make sure that you mention the module, or if it is your dissertation that they are supporting you with, then that, so that your tutor can place you.

Emails are now the most frequent form of communication, with some tutors needing to blow the cobwebs off the telephone before answering it. Because of this, your tutors are likely to receive anything from 20 to 200 emails in any one day, so please avoid sending any that are unnecessary. Please do not use your tutor as your own private version of 'Ask Jeeves.' Consider, before contacting your tutor, whether the information that you are requesting might be found elsewhere. Is it in your course handbook? Might it be in the module outline? Is it in the library of information that your module tutor has put onto your virtual learning environment (VLE) for you? Avoid asking your tutor as an *easier* alternative to checking the guidance literature that has been produced for you: always check the literature, first. Another consideration is whether you are raising a query about an area that your tutor actually holds any responsibility for – something which we explore in the next section on building 'useful relationships'.

There is a final point that is worth mentioning. Your tutors will really appreciate it if you make clear that you understand that you are not their only priority. Phrases such as 'I appreciate that you are really busy, but …' or 'If you could possibly find the time' will in all likelihood engender a great deal more goodwill than an email sent in the evening and demanding a response by the next day. As a general rule, unless your course handbook or tutor specifies otherwise, you should allow around five working days for your email to be answered. This allows for the many other responsibilities that your supervisor or tutor may have in addition to teaching, which are discussed below. If they have not replied within those five days, then it is worth sending a polite reminder, just in case your message has become lost in a sea of emails. If you are eager for a response in relation to your work and your tutor does not reply with as much haste as you would like, please do not be tempted to ask a range of other tutors. There are two reasons why this is a bad idea. The first is that you are triplicating the time and attention given to you, in an already demanding environment (we shall shortly discuss the dynamics of this more fully). The second is that, in all probability, you will get as many different answers as the different people you have asked. Academic work is highly subjective, with a huge variance in perceptions. Your tutor understands what you are doing best, and will be assessing the finished piece. Be patient and wait for feedback from them so as to avoid muddying any waters.

Face-to-face tutorials

The role of the academic tutor has changed beyond recognition in recent years.

There is no tutor who sits doing the crossword in-between occasional visits from tutees. On any given day, many tutors will be juggling planning and preparation, teaching, review and feedback on work, marking and uploading of grades and feedback, their own research and writing commitments, individual tutorials, committee meetings, planning meetings, team and staff development meetings, marketing and administrative requirements (Student Example 3.1). They are also likely to have commitments outside of the university, such as reviewing for journals, acting in a consultancy role or regulating the marking on a different university course as an external examiner. Now, this does not mean that they will not have time for you. On the contrary, students are tutors' first priority, but you should be aware that their time may not be as 'flexible' as you might think it is. It is highly likely that exactly five minutes after finishing your tutorial they will be rushing off to a meeting or to teach or that they will have another tutorial booked in. If you need to rearrange a tutorial for genuine reasons, then try to do that as far in advance as possible in order to work around busy schedules.

Student example 3.1   Changing a tutorial appointment

Lucy had arranged to see her tutor on her Advanced Management module to discuss her upcoming assignment. She woke up later than expected and did not think that she would be able to get all the way to university for her 10 a.m. tutorial. She sent a quick email, just before 10 a.m., asking whether she could change it to the next day instead. She was somewhat put out when the tutor explained that their next available slot was not for 10 days, as that was really close to her assignment deadline.

It goes without saying that this does not refer to those situations where circumstances beyond your control, such as a family crisis or genuine illness, prevent you from attending a meeting at the last minute. But it will be very useful for you to always work on the premise that time is precious. Arrange tutorials well in advance and be punctual so that you can make full use of your time. Previously prepared notes, questions or an informal 'agenda' will really help to keep your time focused. You need to guard the one-to-one time that you spend with your tutor carefully and aim to gain the very most from it. Do not forget that hours spent reading and feeding back on your work are likely to count as allocated time, too.

When difficulties arise

Before we go on to the much wider raft of individuals who are there to support you with your studies, it is necessary to consider what you should do if you feel that your relationship with your tutor is problematic, particularly in the case of research supervision, where that tutor will be your key support for a number of years. It is worth acknowledging from the outset that you may not gel with your tutor instantly, so do allow for that. If at first things seem a little bit strained, it may be a case of wires being crossed or meanings being misinterpreted; you may simply need time to get used to each other. So, seek clarification of any confusions that you may have and allow a few meetings or correspondences for your relationship with your tutor to become established. If you have allowed time and things still do not seem right, then it is good to seek some advice rather than struggle on. Here, it is good to be aware of available channels of communication and support. You will, in all likelihood, have a fellow student on your course who is a course representative of some description, someone who you can speak to in confidence. Although this individual may not be able to rectify any difficulties themselves, they should be able to direct you to somebody who can. Have you been allocated a personal tutor who is there to support your pastoral needs? Your personal tutor, or mentor, will be your most sympathetic ear. If there is not someone of this ilk, then there may be other tutors who will be happy to talk through any issues with you and give some guidance. Of course, if you have more serious concerns, you may want to go directly to your course leader, a manager within your graduate school, to someone from student services or maybe even to a representative from the Students' Union. What is most important here is that you should never feel that you are struggling with a problem in isolation – there are a number of avenues that you can take for helpful advice and assistance. Check your university guidance, which may include a student charter, for the support that is available to you.

Often, the issues that arise can be easily dissipated, originating from misinterpretation or misunderstanding, but it is still helpful to get assistance before they escalate. However, there may be occasions when changes need to be made and your tutors will be happy to explore these options with you.

Other useful relationships

Universities have a number of staff employed to make your experience as worthwhile and as enjoyable as possible. There are experts to support your use of the library and its resources, to enable you to register on the modules that you want to take and to help you to sort out your finances. These are mentioned as the three most closely related to your studies, but your student services will have an expansive list of further support services available. Make the most of the expertise that is available in each field. Do not be afraid to make contact with individuals whom you do not really know; either they will be able to help you or they will be happy to point you in the direction of someone else who can.

One of the most useful relationships that you can establish is with your subject librarian (Student Example 3.2). This incredible individual can help you to find your way around complex search engines, track down elusive publications and can even help you with using and referencing the literature in you work. Their job is not to tidy up bookshelves, but to support you in the resources aspect of your study. Get to know them and make maximum use of their expert knowledge. Most librarians will allow you to book a session with them, where you can make clear your specific needs and where they can help to point you in the right direction. If studying as a research student, then your resource needs are likely to be very specific, and your librarian will be a great help in locating the necessary theoretical literature.

Student example 3.2   Advice from your subject librarian

Manjit was exploring a very specific dissertation area for her MA in Sociology. It was about the role that artwork played in the nineteenth century in bringing a greater understanding of medical sciences to a wider public. She was really struggling to find any resources to support her work other than a small range of medical textbooks. When she arranged a meeting with her subject librarian, the librarian told her about the range of resources that could be found at the Wellcome Institute Collection in London. She also advised her to arrange some time with the History and Art librarians at her own library, as these areas all overlapped in her particular area of study.

Who is responsible for your course in Registry? Find out. This is the person to contact with queries about when you need to register for your modules, or, if you want to change a module, to switch from full-time to part-time, or, perhaps, to intercalate (take a break from your studies, discussed further in Chapter 8). They also deal with the assessment and grade side of things. So, if you need to know what grade you require in your final assessment to achieve a Distinction, these are the people to help you. Very like the Queen, your tutors do not deal with any matters involving money. So, if you have queries involving payments and costs, you will be most successful going straight to Finance, who deal with this element of your studies.

Who is the administrator for your course? The administrators oversee the running of your course and so can help you with finding documents, people, rooms and deadlines. If you are not sure who you need to contact with a query, then the course administrator is a good place to start. Your postgraduate study is very like a high street which is home to many different stores, serving many different purposes. In the same way, you have a whole institute or department with a wide range of knowledge and expertise at your disposal. You are not going to go into the bakers and ask them where the paracetamol are, or whether they can order that new book on photography for you. In the same way, you would not ask someone in Finance about ordering a journal article. You seek what you need from the most suitable source. Your tutor is not a one-stop-shop. Your tutor's job is the teaching element, and for many tutors the sophistications of Finance, Registry or the interlibrary loan system remain a mystery, so go directly to those people who know best.

Peer learning and online communities

It is probable that your most tangible sources of support at university will not be those who are employed there, but your peers. Your peers understand the pressures that you experience or the confusion that you may feel at times. In all likelihood, you will all have obtained 'bits' of information from a wide range of sources that will be useful to one another. Be sure to share them. If you have worries or are anxious about expectations, then it is highly unlikely that you are the only one. Do not be afraid to be open with your peers. When you do this, it is likely that you will discover that all of those apprehensions that you thought were felt by you alone are, in fact, commonplace. One problem of further study is that, quite contrary to feeling 'advanced' in your thinking, you can become painfully aware of just how much you do not know. As we tried to reassure you in Chapter 1, this is perfectly normal: do not be afraid to talk about how you are feeling. There will be many friendly ears if you are feeling overwhelmed, as we have all felt the same way at some point.

The importance of sharing with your peers does not only apply to the administrative or the pastoral side of your course, it also relates to the content and your own knowledge development. As a research student, this may happen within your 'desk environment' (very often, postgraduate study areas are shared) or within additional training opportunities or research group meetings. As a research student, it is very easy to feel isolated, as only you are undertaking that particular area of research. It is important to realise, though, that your 'learning as a research student' experience is a shared one. You will encounter similar experiences in areas such as choices of methodology, resources or interaction with research participants, regardless of subject area, and it is good to share what you learn as it helps you to develop your understanding. This is further explored in Chapter 5.

If you are studying on a taught module, then you should make the most of every opportunity to interact with your peers. As a tutor, there is nothing more satisfying than observing students sharing knowledge and ideas, finding mutual points of reference, suggesting related literature or, most importantly, challenging one another. Constructive criticism will become an important part of your academic development and you need to see this as a positive, as it helps you to consider different perspectives. Although, with your own research in particular, the process may sometimes feel very isolating, the creation of knowledge should be a communal activity. Engeström (2001: 137) describes the new windows of opportunity, or the 'third spaces' that open up when new collaborations are formed. And Luca (2009: 13) celebrates the 'illumination' that happens when two minds meet. The more collaborations you establish, the greater the opportunities for a rich exchange of knowledge and the creation of new ideas. If you are only interacting with literature and your tutor and not with those who are sharing a similar learning experience, then you are passing up the opportunity to learn from a whole wealth of alternative perceptions and experiences.

These interactions do not only take place in a classroom environment. If your course is not taught through face-to-face sessions, then you are likely to be offered opportunities for exchanging ideas through online discussion boards. These can be a wonderful means of sharing, reflecting, reconsidering and unpacking, but, and this may seem ridiculously obvious, only if students engage. It is very difficult for tutors to prompt and cajole students into discussion in an online environment in the same way that they might do face to face. Initiative on your part is needed. At first, you may need to get past the fear of saying anything that you think might make you look 'stupid'. Clearly, the dynamics change when you are typing up something that will remain evident for the duration of the course, in comparison with making a passing comment in a classroom that will be quickly forgotten. But, if that were always the case, then no one would ever publish anything, as our thinking constantly moves on. McNiff (2010) wisely warns us to 'hold on to our knowledge lightly', because what we thought we knew yesterday could, in all likelihood, turn out to be wrong tomorrow. It is entirely possible to be mistaken, and that is fine. You are not expected to make profound statements on an online discussion board, rather you are expected to ask questions or to comment and add to a point that someone else has made. This should not be too intimidating. Become more involved and you might find that you are happy to initiate new discussions. These forums can be a rich source of new ideas and stimulating information. The fact that they remain means that you can always go back and revisit points that were raised and they are a useful source of information when the time comes to formulate an assessment piece.

Studying at postgraduate level is a strange conundrum. Although you have reached a point where you are viewed as having a certain level of 'expertise', it is highly likely that you will begin to feel less confident about your knowledge than you have ever felt previously. That is normal. As you become more advanced in your thinking, you become increasingly aware of the complex nature of 'knowledge' and of its intangible qualities. You come to realise that there is no one answer, just a myriad of viewpoints, and that it is impossible to be aware of them all. That is fine, because you do not need to be aware of them all. The reason that you have become a postgraduate student is because you have learned how to study and how to question effectively, not because you have all the answers. We further explore some of these issues in Chapter 5.

But do not forget that the absolutely best place for a stimulating chat, if at all possible, is over coffee. You do not always have to be on your academic guard, allow yourself time just to chat about anything other than your work every now and again. Take time to get to know your peers in an informal sense.

Being open and honest develops trust, and trusting relationships scaffold your mental health and well-being.

Time management

Regardless of the particular circumstances that impact upon your postgraduate studies, you are likely to come across challenges. It may be that you are studying in addition to your regular full-time job and perhaps even in addition to caring for a family. If this is the case, then it is vital that you timetable regular periods for study into your week. You (and perhaps your family) need to become used to these regular episodes of study, otherwise they will be put off until tomorrow, and tomorrow and tomorrow. Study must become a habitual aspect of your life if you are going to be able to give it anything close to the time needed. You will have to become slightly selfish in this aspect and remember that it is only short term. Timetable study sessions at a time that best suits you and your lifestyle. Everyone has different peaks and troughs to their alertness and concentration, so make sure that you are studying at a time when you can be 'switched on'. If you are overly tired or distracted, then the time you spend sat in front of the computer will be fruitless. Remember that your study time is about quality not quantity.

It may be that you are now enjoying the luxury of full-time education with no work commitments. This can have its own complications, particularly if you have come from a very structured and rigidly timetabled environment. The prospect of having a largely empty diary that you need to utilise in the best way possible can be rather disconcerting. Where do you start? Start with any taught sessions or tutorials that you have and work around that. It is really useful to have study time after taught sessions in order to follow up on ideas that have been raised and identify appropriate resources. You will need time to be at your computer, but be very clear about what that time is for. Is it for searching for appropriate literature, for reading, for writing, for analysis or for completing set learning tasks? Be clear about what the aim of the session is so as to avoid the 'deer caught in the headlights' times when you really do not know where to start.

If you are a research student carrying out fieldwork, then your timetable will need to be organised around that, allowing plenty of time for preparation and follow-up. You need to be extremely well prepared for any visits to the field, but, equally important, is your time to reflect and write up notes after the time working with your research participants. Particularly if you are making field notes or undertaking observations, your mind will be full of information after leaving the field and it is vital to allow time to unwind by getting it all written down. This will be an essential part of your data collection, so try your utmost to allow time for it.

A word of warning is to make sure that you do not suffer 'burnout' from too many long sessions sat in front of your computer or in the library. You should treat your study like a job and allocate time to it, but not allow it to overwhelm your life entirely. You still need 'time out' to be you, to be with your family or to socialise, to do sport, to be active. Allow downtime, where you meet with friends and discuss anything other than your research. This is a necessity: you need breaks from your study in order to be able to return to it with renewed enthusiasm.

Whose work is it anyway?

Student example 3.3   Publishing and academic etiquette

John's PhD bridged two different disciplines (and centres): Education and Sports. As a result, he sat in something of a no-man's land between the qualitative/constructivist approach taken by Education and the positivist/scientific approach taken by Sport. His natural leaning was towards the former (views and opinions were the key focus for him), but at various points he was urged to have more convincing sets of statistics to underpin his data. An expert from the Sports Department attempted to enculturate John into systems such as Statistical Package for the Social Sciences (SPSS), but to no avail. The nature of his work (and his very nature) was constructivist.

A year or so into his PhD studies, John had his first publication, a very basic discussion piece about the changing approaches happening in the Education landscape, a product of his literature review. Sometime later, he encountered the SPSS tutor from Sports and was taken aback when the tutor made a barbed comment about the fact that John had not included him as a co-author on the published discussion piece. John felt racked with guilt that he had broken a cardinal sin of academic etiquette.

What are your thoughts on this (Student Example 3.3)? For many undertaking postgraduate study, as we have already touched upon, the inherent insecurity of the role would cause the student to believe that the fault lies entirely with them. This is most certainly not the case. For any MA or PhD supervisor, the hours that they spend discussing and editing work with the student are part and parcel of their role as 'teacher'. What the student then does with the knowledge that they develop through the relationship is up to them. As has been stated earlier, frank honesty is key to any academic relationship. If a tutor would like to share a publication with you, then they should ask your view on this. If they are requesting equal ownership of your academic work (co-authorship), then you should be treated as an equal in this process. In our experience across Education, Management and Professional Studies, the norm would then be that the postgraduate student would be the designated first author and the tutor the second author. What is important is that you feel sufficiently confident to say a firm 'No' if you do not agree that the content is theirs and you would prefer to continue individually. Alternatively, you may feel appreciative having their support when first embarking for the arena of publication and happy to share authorship; but the choice must remain yours. If you are unsure of the expectations within your own supervisory context, then simply ask.

Of course, this concept of the ownership of knowledge, known as intellectual property rights (IPRs), will be quite different in situations where the student has specifically been employed as a research assistant. In this case, where the student is working alongside the tutor on a shared research project, the intellectual copyright of any publications should be established through a contract at the outset of the project. In all likelihood, any work at all that is produced outside of the student's PhD will be done so on a shared basis, as a research 'team'.

Key ideas and terms

Establishing shared expectations should happen at the outset of your studies so that you are clear about what is expected of you and what to expect of others.

Professional communication should always be maintained between academic staff and students. Leave text-speak for your friends.

It is fine to ask because you are not expected to know. If you are new to the course and the university, then there will be an awful lot to get to grips with.

Seek help from those who know best. Become familiar with those who have responsibility in various areas and make maximum use of their expertise.

Share information and ideas with your peers. Learning does not need to be a solitary activity: share, inspire and be inspired.

Take time to create friendships because this develops trust, which develops security.

'Hold knowledge lightly' is a wonderful phrase to remember. Knowledge is transient, forever in flux. Do not be afraid of being wrong, just present your view at that moment in time. Your views will change as your knowledge develops.

Intellectual property rights (IPRs) refers to the 'ownership' of academic works that are produced and published.

Chapter summary

In this chapter, we have explored the highs and lows of creating and sustaining useful relationships during your time as a postgraduate student. This type of information is unlikely to be found in any other reference book and is unlikely to be openly discussed. But, there is a reason why these discussions should not be overlooked, and that is because the aspect of relationships is just as important as any other in ensuring that your time in higher education is successful. In fact, the relationships that you create could make or break your whole study experience. It is good to have an idea of how to approach your academic relationships from experienced tutors. It is also helpful to know what you can do if things do not go according to plan. The most important thing to be clear about is that it is absolutely okay not to understand and also to ask. No one will think any less of you for that. If things do not seem to be going as you had hoped, then it is okay to question. If things do not *seem* to be going right, then it probably means that there is, in fact, something wrong, and that some sort of intervention is needed.

You have a whole host of people who will be willing to go out of their way to make your time as a postgraduate student a successful one. The important thing is to be brave enough to build relationships with them in order to best utilise their support. The saying, 'It's not what you know but who you know,' is very true, and applies to the area of postgraduate study in exactly the same way as any other. However, whilst building relationships and working hard at your research, remember to keep some time for yourself and those who are important to you.

4

Reading to Some Purpose

Chapter overview

This chapter covers a central skill for all postgraduate students: reading. Many postgraduates struggle with the reading required for their course. This is partly due to the sheer volume of reading required by some course tutors for their modules, but it is often down to not knowing how to read to some purpose. This chapter will help you with reading to some purpose. In this case, the reading is to engage with the theoretical and policy literature that will form the essential background for your studies and your writing. Reading to some purpose is a skill or technique that can be learnt. And just as some children take longer than others to learn to read, so some students find it easier than others to read to some purpose. But all can benefit from giving some attention to why they are reading, how to take in and record what they have read, and how to deconstruct the theoretical literature that provides the core knowledge base for their course.

Thinking to some purpose

Just before the Second World War, a British philosopher called L. Susan Stebbing (1939) wrote a manual of first aid to enable clear thinking, titled *Thinking to Some Purpose*, which showed how to detect illogical thought in other people's mental processes and how to avoid them in our own.

Published on the eve of the war, she argued:

> There is an urgent need to-day for the citizens of a democracy to think well. It is not enough to have freedom of the Press and parliamentary institutions.

> Our difficulties are due partly to our own stupidity, partly to the exploitation of that stupidity, and partly to our own prejudices and personal desires ... We easily fall into the habit of accepting compressed statements which save us from the trouble of thinking. Thus arises what I shall call Potted Thinking ... This metaphor seems to me to be appropriate, because potted thinking is easily accepted, is concentrated in form, and has lost the vitamins essential to mental nourishment ... A potted belief should be the outcome of a belief that is not potted. It should not be held on to when circumstances have changed and new factors have come to light ... the critical questioning at times of our potted beliefs is necessary for the development of our capacity to think to some purpose. (Stebbing, 1939: 53)

This metaphor of **potted thinking**, as opposed to original critical thinking, underpins much of our advice in this book on how to succeed as a postgraduate student. And the principle applies very much to the approach to reading that we will recommend you take. As Stebbing suggests in the above quote, we should be aiming to keep our minds open to fresh ideas, and especially to seek an original and creative approach to the reading that will be required for your course.

The majority of taught postgraduate courses have a modular structure. As we mentioned in Chapter 2, each module will have its own resource list, which will be mostly made up of book chapters and journal articles relevant to the course. Occasionally, there will be hundreds of such references given, but more usually there will be one or two dozen listed references. It is important to understand that the given references are simply a starting point. They are not, and cannot be, an exhaustive list of everything you could read to support your study and to bring into your written assignment(s) for the module. To understand this, let us return to the idea of thinking to some purpose.

The modules that comprise your course reflect the main areas that the course designers (who are most likely your tutors) consider are the core components to your field of study. Their purpose is to introduce the separate areas of study that together combine to describe and define the field of study. As such, therefore, the modules themselves can only be introductory illustrative examples of what academics currently consider represents the field of study. So, for you, the postgraduate student, the modules and the reading that goes with each are beginnings, jumping-off points, from which you must find your own direction and path of understanding. And this, your path of understanding, will be what gives the module its purpose for you. To achieve the highest grades in the module is simply a matter of finding a path that has some purpose for you. This purpose may be a link to your professional work, or to ideas that you have developed earlier as an undergraduate or perhaps in another module. The main thing is that you will have redefined the module in terms of your own purpose, which has meaning and significance for you.

This is what will now shape and guide your reading for the module. You can take the module in a direction that is personal to you, find and express your voice within the broad topic of the module, and support your view and argument with reading that is relevant to it (Student Example 4.1).

> ## Student example 4.1   The tutor's point of view
>
> Think about this from the point of view of the tutor. Let us say that there are a dozen recommended texts for a module. She is marking two assignments on broadly the same topic. Taylor's work only uses the references given in the module contract (perhaps suggesting potted thinking), whereas Lemar uses one or two of these but supplements them with references that are current and relevant to the module but not supplied by the tutor. Which assignment will be more interesting for the tutor? Tutors are human and will mark more highly work that is interesting, fresh and original.

Approaches to reading

In the last section, we uncovered the importance of thinking about how the module has purpose for you as a postgraduate student. Thinking in this way will influence your choice of reading and lead you to use the reading list as a jumping-off point to explore your own personal connection with the module theme(s). In this section, we examine some different kinds of reading that will be needed for successful postgraduate work, and make clear the different approaches needed for each. We will use some technical terms that we have coined in order to illustrate three broad reading approaches that will save you time, focus your thinking, and organise your reading for your assignments and dissertation.

These terms are: **meta-reading, meso-reading and micro-reading**. The terms come from ancient Greek, with 'meta-' connoting a higher level or overview, 'meso-' deriving from the Greek word for 'middle', and 'micro-' from the Greek word meaning 'small'. So, meta-reading is taking a broad sweep of the areas or themes comprising the module; meso-reading is looking at each area or theme within the module; and micro-reading is taking an in-depth look at one or no more than two of those areas or themes.

Meta-reading will be used to get the gist of the module. If you are fortunate, one of the books on the reading list will be tagged as a key text and will give a good overview of the module. You do not need to read this text in detail, but use it to give you an idea of what the module covers, its range and the topics within it, and as a source for further reading aligned to whatever purpose you decide the module has for you (see the section above on 'Thinking to Some Purpose').

Meso-reading will be used to decide which themes of the module have potential to give it purpose for you. These will be books and articles that explore different aspects and themes of the module. You may scour four or five themes before you decide on which one best suits your purpose. A good tip is to give articles priority over books. They are shorter, are often more current, and can help you cover a lot of ground in a short time. It is easier and far more practical to read five articles than five books.

Micro-reading will be used once you have settled on the theme that best suits your purpose. There may be one or two articles or books in the module reading list that hit the spot, but more likely you will source these yourself, quite possibly from references in the meso-reading that you have done, which then guides you towards more specialist resources on your special topic within the module. Internet sources are more likely to appear in your micro-reading than either meso-reading or meta-reading. These sources can be very valuable – original, up to date and authoritative if penned by established and credible authorities, possibly academics who blog, or specialists in their field.

DRAWING 4.1   Reading in bed

The point here is that your work will be enhanced if you organise and control your reading for each module (Student Example 4.2), which is an important part of your self-management that we identified as essential for successful postgraduate study in Chapter 1.

Student example 4.2   Reading for an assignment

Mai is doing the reading for her module in Research Methods in Social Science. Her meta-reading comprises one book recommended by the tutor that gives a wide overview of the topic; her meso-reading is one further book and three journal articles on the philosophical basis of different approaches to research methodology; and her micro-reading is 15 different sources on methods of special interest to her, which are Life History and Narrative Research in Education, including book chapters, journal articles and Web sources. So, her reading totals up to around 20 or so academic references to support an assignment – which is both respectable and manageable.

Doing literature searches

By using the 'meta-/meso-/micro-' approach to reading to some purpose, we have given ourselves a potential structure for one of the key components of a postgraduate dissertation or thesis: the literature review (see the section below on 'Dealing with Theoretical Literature', and the section in Chapter 7 on 'Research Questions'). By 'literature', we incorporate all reading matter, including books, articles and online material, as well as documents that are sourced from institutions and government departments, sometimes called **grey literature**. This last one is a useful resource for most assignments and dissertations. Familiarity with relevant grey literature demonstrates to the assessors that you have delved more deeply into your topic of study, and that you are able to call on up-to-date sources in order to utilise policy documents or in-house manuals, texts and documents that will give your study a contemporaneous and authentic feel.

The starting point for your **literature search** in modules should always be the module resource list that is provided as part of the module contract. This will contain both meta- and meso-reading sources, and, as noted above, these will be the places to start for your own personalised literature searches.

For your dissertation (see Chapter 7), the literature search will be more dynamic, more influenced by your own interests and personal take on the topic of study. In some cases, your dissertation topic will have been influenced by a sub-topic within a module that might have been the subject of a unit of study within the module, and covered by one or more lectures. In this case, there will be given sources to accompany that unit – again, you should be thinking of these as jumping-off points for your own search.

In the next section, 'Accessing Literature Online', we explain how to make the best use of the internet in order to find literature to support your study. But there are a number of sources other than the Web that will be useful to explore.

A very good but often overlooked source of effective current literature on academic topics is the **academic journal 'special issue'**. All academic areas spawn journals that exist to provide outlets for academic work in an accessible and current form. Academic journals are published regularly, some of them as often as each month, but more usually four or six times a year. Most journals make use of special issues that are organised on a particular theme or topic within the academic area. Examples for the field of Education are: blended learning, work-based research, leadership in post-compulsory education. You can find special issues by searching the website of journals that cover your subject area – they will be listed there. Special issues are valuable because they bring together different perspectives and angles on a single topic, so each one will be both potentially valuable in itself as well as a source of further relevant literature through the list of references that are given at the end of each article.

Another good but overlooked source of current literature is the **academic conference**. Your tutors should be aware of those that take place, usually annually, in the academic area that you are interested in. It is unlikely that you will find a single conference that consists solely of topics relevant to your study, but even quite general conferences, such as those organised in Education by the British Educational Research Association (BERA), will have themes or strands running through them that will attract a number of conference contributors who are working in your area of interest.

A third neglected source of good literature consists of the websites or blogs of academics who specialise in your subject area. You will become familiar with the names that recur as you become increasingly knowledge-able about your topic through your general reading. Look up these people via Google and you will be directed to their university website, on which they will have a page that lists all their academic work, and possibly a link to their own blog that will contain further references to work that they like to share.

Exactly because these three methods – journal special issues, academic conferences and **writers' blogs** – are less popular sources in postgraduate work, using them will bring your work an originality, depth and presence that will help you stand apart from the crowd. It will demonstrate to the assessors that you have the initiative and motivation to search a little more in depth, and that you are committed to discovering original sources and new knowledge that will lend authenticity and immediacy to your own work.

Accessing literature online

Here, we want to emphasise again (as in the Chapter 2 section on 'Using the Library', and the Chapter 3 section on 'Other Useful Relationships') the valuable benefit of using your university library and, in particular, the **specialist subject librarian**. They are not only experts on identifying and sourcing relevant academic texts for your work, but are also experts on carrying out online internet library catalogue searches. They receive module resource lists from subject tutors and will help you track down the items that you are interested in.

However, we recognise that, sometimes, time, circumstances or geography can make access to libraries and librarians difficult. Fortunately, there is now such an array of Web-based resources for the university student that it has become much easier to track down suitable material yourself. The first step is to ensure that your university online profile is up to date, i.e. your username and password. Through your university portal, you will be able to access an online version of your university catalogue that may have a name such as 'Summon'. Via this, you can search for all the online resources to which your university is subscribed, which will include most of the popular journals in your academic area and in related fields of study, as well as academic books, reports and other grey literature.

The commonest way of carrying out this initial literature search is to search by **key terms** (Student Example 4.3 and see also the section in Chapter 5 on 'How to Research and Use Key Terms').

Student example 4.3   Key terms in your search

Olivia is planning her assignment for an Education Policy module. She decides on her topic, which is: 'University College Partnerships and Widening Participation: Insights from a Small-Scale Case Study of One University and Its College Partners'. She logically takes her key terms for her online library catalogue search from the main title: 'University College Partnerships' and 'Widening Participation'. The use of the inverted commas is crucial, because they ensure that the search is made for 'University College Partnerships' and not, say, just 'Partnerships', which would extend the search too widely for it to be useful.

We recommend that, no matter how far you may be from your university library, you make an appointment with the subject librarian, who will be able to show you tips and techniques to make your online library catalogue searches more effective. This investment in time and trouble will repay itself many times over in helping you understand how these systems work and to avoid wasted searches.

Using the online search, you will be able to do two extremely valuable things. First, you will be able to track down whether your university has in stock any key book texts that you may want to use and refer to in your study, and also where those texts are shelved in the library. Second, you will be able to track down the most relevant journal articles for your study. You should be making more use of these than of book sources. The reasons for this are that: they will often be more up to date; they will contain relevant material in a concise form, whereas books tend to present information more expansively; they will enable you to draw from a wide range of sources, whereas there may only be a limited number of books relevant to your area of study; they are frequently downloadable as full-text articles, so that you can save them on your laptop or PC.

What about *Wikipedia*? Our view is that *Wikipedia* is a useful resource for signposting information. Because it is so comprehensive and accessible, it is a good way to quickly gain an overview of a person, movement, or topic. However, and it is a big however, *Wikipedia* is not an infallible source and its coverage very much reflects the contributor's take on the entry. There is no peer-review process in place and, as a result, we advise that you use it with care. It is almost never advisable or acceptable to reference *Wikipedia* as an authoritative source in your work.

Highlighting and note-taking

If your funds allow, we strongly recommend that you print off the most relevant articles and sections from books, especially from your meta- and meso-reading, but also from your micro-reading, if possible. There is nothing like having the full text of an article in front of you to enable you to fully understand its relevance and to select out potential quotes that you can use to support your thesis or argument. We recommend that you use a highlighter pen to mark these out – this will save time later and makes comparing and collating reading material so much easier.

Of course, you may prefer to do this electronically, and the most common word-processing software, Microsoft Word, offers the capability of highlighting text using coloured blocks. Each to their own, and there is no right or wrong about this, so we suggest that you maybe try both systems and go for the one that suits you best. As well as highlighting in colour, either physically or electronically, we recommend that you get into the habit of marking up your printed or saved texts with your own comments and notes. This is really good practice as it allows you to call up the relevance of a sentence or paragraph long after you have had the original thought about it. And doing this will help to generate interesting phrases and sentences that you will be able to use in your assignment or dissertation.

Taking inspiration from the title of this chapter, 'Reading to Some Purpose', by highlighting and note-taking, you will be able to make maximum use of your reading and translate your ideas into useable material for your written work. As we have emphasised throughout this book, our aim is to help you become a reflective and critical reader and writer, and avoid potted thinking. One way in which you can bring this to life in practice is when you come across two academic authors who hold different, contrasting or even opposing views and opinions: juxtapose these and add your own opinion (Student Example 4.4).

Student example 4.4   Taking opinions together

Lucas's Education dissertation has the following paragraph:

> Smith (2012: 37) concludes that mature students may be disadvantaged in higher education through 'the absence of relevant cultural capital and attendant associations with the education system into which they aspire', whereas Jones (2010) has suggested that older learners can with benefit bring a different set of experiences to their learning experience. Juxtaposing opinions suggests that we should not accept too rigid a definition of cultural capital that excludes other relevant experience and associations that have the potential to prepare older learners for advanced study.

In Student Example 4.4, Lucas has identified two authors, Smith and Jones, who have contrasting views about how prepared mature students can be for higher education. He has added his own opinion that, in effect, suggests that Smith may be taking an over-rigid, deterministic view of cultural capital, whereas Jones acknowledges that these students may bring additional skills and experiences into the mix. Also note, in passing, that because Lucas has given an actual quote from Smith, it is necessary to give the page number of the reference. Because he has paraphrased Jones's view, following his university's referencing system, he does not have to give a page number.

Dealing with theoretical literature

On a taught postgraduate course, the articles and books that are recommended for reading alongside the various modules together comprise the **theoretical literature** for the area of study. This literature is subdivided into topics or themes, just as the course is subdivided into modules. So, in the same way as we thought about reading for the course, we can think of theoretical literature as meta-literature (relating to the whole course), meso-literature (relating to the module) and micro-literature (relating to your chosen area of study or topic within the module).

So, the theoretical literature for an assignment within a module is likely to comprise one or two general texts, several articles or books on the general area of the assignment and then perhaps a dozen more in-depth articles particularly relevant to the specific topic you have chosen for your assignment. The theoretical literature for a dissertation will reflect a similar pattern, with some general texts and some books and articles on broad themes relevant to your topic, but the majority would be articles covering detailed aspects of your study alongside relevant grey literature.

Many students worry about how complicated some theoretical literature can seem. Often, these concerns are down to being unfamiliar with the terminology of the subject or discipline. This aspect can be controlled through finding a good work of meta-literature that comprehensively describes the field of study and goes through ideas and terms, explaining them for the non-specialist. Particularly good texts of this kind are produced by the Open University (OU) for their students, and an OU text on your subject area may be an excellent starting point for getting to grips with the theoretical literature for your module. Sometimes, module reading lists will contain a good overview text. The important thing is not to suffer in silence, so do not be afraid to ask for advice from tutors, subject librarians and other students. Talking through difficult territory with your student peers is a great way of diluting the fear that can build up through not comprehending the concepts and ideas on which a module is built.

Also, a word of advice. Sometimes, academic writers themselves fail to appreciate how inaccessible their work can be for the reader. This can arise where the academic is writing with other academics and researchers in mind rather than students who may be less familiar with the discipline. So, if a piece of theoretical literature seems complex, obscure, technical or in other ways inaccessible, it could well be down to the writing itself rather than you, the reader. There is an old academic joke, 'eschew obfuscation' – in other words, write simply. Unfortunately, too many scholars do not heed this good advice, so be prepared to dump inaccessible theoretical texts, or at least read summaries or simplified versions first if that work is a necessary part of your study. Be reassured, there will almost certainly be alternative sources available that will be far more useful.

In both module assignments and the dissertation, it is the theoretical literature that will define the conceptual framework for the study. **Conceptual framework** is a term that is often used quite loosely and interchangeably with **theoretical framework** to mean the broad conceptual or theoretical approach that you are taking, for example positivist, interpretivist, feminist, biographical, critical theory and so on. It is not necessary to pin your colours to any one single conceptual framework – it is often safer and more accurate to describe your study as 'drawing upon' two or more theoretical traditions, allowing you, in turn, to use a mixed methods approach to planning your study and to data collection.

As we make clear in Chapter 7, when it comes to the dissertation, your aims, objectives and research questions will have arisen in the light of your reading of the theoretical literature, in combination with your own ideas, professional knowledge and experience. In your literature review, you will need to define and challenge the main points of view described in the literature, concepts and terminology that you will use. While the perspective that you adopt for your study and the concepts that you apply will be derived from the work of other writers, it will become the basis of your own theoretical framework that you will apply to your chosen topic or area of study.

Saving and filing articles and reports

Whether you prefer to archive your documents electronically or use a paper filing system, some method of saving these sources and organising them so that you can easily find the ones you want when you need them is essential. Most people use a combination of electronic and paper storage, so we will consider each in turn.

Filing paper sources is quite straightforward as long as you have a system that you follow consistently. We recommend filing articles, reports and book chapters in alphabetical order of the author's surname. Author surname is the method that academics use to refer to another author's work, for example Smith (2016). In this example, Smith is the author surname and 2016 is the year of publication of the article or chapter. The full reference will be located at the end of the article. In a book chapter, the full reference may be at the end of the chapter or at the end of the book. Either way, all references will be listed in alphabetical order of author surname, including corporate authors such as Cabinet Office or Health and Safety Executive, so it makes sense to use this system for your own filing of printed texts.

The same principle applies to electronic storage. When you save an article or chapter, name it according to the author and date, so in our example above the file name becomes 'Smith 2016'. If Smith wrote two articles or chapters in 2016, name the first one 'Smith 2016a' and the second one 'Smith 2016b'. This is the standard practice when listing references at the end of any piece of academic work, so it makes sense to use this system for your own filing purposes.

A useful system is to organise your articles and book chapters into themes. This involves creating a folder for each theme and then saving the articles and books for that theme into the relevant folder. This system will enable you to track down all the references that you have found useful on any of the themes relevant to your topic of study. It also has the advantage of allowing you to see whether you have enough sources for each of your themes or whether you might need to search out any more.

We should underline this last paragraph because it is about backing up your electronic data. Under no circumstances rely on your PC, laptop or memory stick without making a **back-up file** copy, and bring this up to date at least once a week, or daily if you are creating many files in a given period. Keep back-up copies in different places in case of a computer crash, theft or fire. We have all suffered data loss and it is a heart-breaking experience if there is no back-up copy. Bear in mind that losing your work because you do not have a back-up copy is not considered a justifiable ground for the award of an extension or for an appeal against a fail grade. So, please back up your work regularly. A good way of reminding yourself is to add 'Back up files' as a reminder in your Outlook Calendar or whichever system you use. Make sure that you add the version number and date to the back-up file name so that you know which is the most recently saved folder.

Key ideas and terms

Potted thinking is a metaphor we use to highlight how we should be aiming to keep our minds open to fresh ideas, and especially to seek an original and creative approach to the reading that will be required for your course.

Meta-reading, meso-reading and micro-reading are terms that come from ancient Greek, with meta- connoting a higher level or overview, meso- deriving from the Greek word for 'middle', and micro- from the Greek word meaning 'small'. So, meta-reading is taking a broad sweep of the area(s) or theme(s) comprising the module, meso-reading is looking at each area or theme within the module, and micro-reading is taking an in-depth look at one or no more than two of those areas or themes.

Grey literature is an important source of evidence for researchers, covering documents that are sourced from institutions and government departments.

A **literature search** is a standard element of almost all assignments and dissertations, and its purpose is to track down and enable a **literature review** that will summarise and critique the existing theoretical knowledge in a field.

Academic journal special issues, academic conferences and writers' blogs are all sources that can bring your work an originality, depth and presence that will help you stand apart from the crowd, demonstrating to the assessors that you have the initiative and motivation to search a little more in depth, and that you are committed to discovering original sources and new knowledge that will lend authenticity and immediacy to your own work.

The **specialist subject librarian** is the person who can give invaluable help in identifying and sourcing relevant academic texts for your work, but also help in carrying out online internet library catalogue searches. They receive module resource lists from subject tutors and will help you track down the items that you are interested in.

Key terms are used in literature searches to identify and locate articles, books and other print and electronic sources relevant to a particular area of study. They can be single words or phrases that must be entered using inverted commas.

Theoretical literature describes the body of articles, books and other reading that together comprise the body of knowledge relating to a topic or theme.

Conceptual framework is a term that is often used quite loosely and interchangeably with **theoretical framework** to mean the broad conceptual or theoretical approach that you are taking, for example positivist, interpretivist, feminist, biographical, critical theory and so on.

Back-up files are copies of folders and documents that may comprise drafts, essays, assignments and vital data and source material. Always keep back-up copies on a separate device or data stick, and in a different location, so that in the event of a computer crash, theft or fire a replacement is available. Files should be copied weekly, as a matter of routine.

Chapter summary

In this chapter, we have encouraged you to acquire the technique of reading to some purpose. We have suggested how you might structure your reading and literature search for a module by breaking it down into meta-, meso- and micro-literature. We have focused particularly on the theoretical literature, and given some advice on what to do where this literature is unclear or difficult. Some practical housekeeping advice is offered, including making the all-important back-up files that will save you if you have a computer disaster.

5

The Representation of Thinking at Postgraduate Level

Chapter overview

This chapter provides an overview of what the representation of thinking at postgraduate level should look and feel like. It makes suggestions as to how best to reflect, define, structure, pursue arguments, convince and research. It concludes with how you integrate all of these aspects into one coherent piece. In so doing, it presents you with a challenge to enter into the dynamics of the productive skills of academic writing and speaking. At postgraduate level, the academic language should show your ownership of an informed and confident stance. At the same time, being able to include the different voices that have moulded your thinking is key. The assumption is made that, as you embark on postgraduate work, you join a community of practice with its own conventions and principles and that you articulate your knowledge and experience in this context, gaining recognition and merit as you do so. But how do you do that? This chapter helps unravel these mysteries by focusing on the idea of academic representation.

In order to support this, the chapter considers the central tenets of reflection and criticality. In particular, it enables you to develop analytical, evaluative and integrative sub-skills that support reflection and criticality. All humans are born with these skills, but are they all able to represent these thinking skills effectively and convince a demanding audience? The latter, in the context of this book, is a very established academic audience that abides by the rules and conventions of postgraduate Level 7 and Level 8 criteria.

These criteria have critical reflection at their heart. How do you avoid falling prey to descriptive, unjustified and atomised writing that could impact negatively on your grades?

Positionality and the reflective 'I'

In postgraduate level writing, whether Postgraduate Certificate/Diploma, Master's or doctorate level, you are showing how you learned through the **representation** of learning. You position yourself as a 're-presenter' or 'integrator' of thinking. You need to bring different frames of reference, and many lenses, to bear on the same idea or experience. As you do that, you are 'representing' and that is where academic reflection is different from everyday reflection. When you think as a human being, you reflect on what your senses and your mind perceive, but that thinking may stop at that. It may develop into some new thinking via what is termed 'dialogic' reflection, as you exchange ideas with others. Incidentally, these others could be peers, tutors, mentors or even dead writers whose books and articles you have read and had a **dialogue** with. With academic writing, especially at postgraduate level, you have to go one step further, and consciously translate the dialogic experience for your audience, explicitly setting out the learning that you have achieved. As you do so, you reflect critically about the ideas that have been received/read/discussed and, in a way, re-theorise, or rethink in a new way, shining a lamp on this thinking that has emerged from your critical reflection. One word to remember here is 'represent' or, better still, 're-present'. You re-present the ideas of others with whom you have 'dialogued' critically via the medium of either writing or speaking and the use of stylistic features that support evaluation, analysis and integration.

This is precisely where the **reflective 'I'** fits in. It is the 'I' of a researcher or practitioner writing who has taken into serious account enough solid and trusted evidence for their thinking. This evidence comes in many forms and is not necessarily from books and journals, although in writing at postgraduate level, there is the need to look for such evidence in what is considered robust research. Indeed, academic journals and books are refereed and are more likely to support your arguments than just any magazine that you might pick up somewhere on a train, for example. Having said that, it is sometimes possible to use less trusted sources (for example, the classic *Wikipedia*), but only by researching the links and going back to the sources in order to read them. The same applies to any ideas that you might pick up from a daily newspaper or magazine or other non-academic publication. For practitioners, often the evidence comes in the form of what is called the 'grey literature', such as policy documents, government strategies, professional magazines and research. As long as that is not your only source of knowledge, and as long as you have included other academic sources as well as balanced the arguments, it is quite acceptable to include these sources in your writing (Student Example 5.1).

Student example 5.1   Strengthening the 'grey' evidence

Grace is writing a 3000-word essay about the gender gap in attainment in English KS4. It is perfectly fine for her to include figures from Ofsted, case studies and reports from the Department for Education, and to refer perhaps to a couple of news headlines. However, what strengthens all of that 'grey' evidence is when she integrates the findings from her critical reading of a few academic journal articles relating to primary research on the topic. These articles re-interpret the gender gap in the light of more critical perspectives (such as the social construction of gender in general as well as possibly the 'gendered' nature of the curriculum). These critical perspectives are not always apparent in the grey literature and might lead you to explore further reading on the subject and widen your horizons as well as receive information in a more critical and balanced way.

The reflective 'I' becomes easy when you steer clear of the 'I believe' or, worse, 'I strongly believe' or, worse still, 'in my personal opinion' kind of statements and instead convince your reader that your belief/argument is informed and can be evidenced. It becomes something like: 'in the light of so and so's work and evidence for … I am inclined to suggest that … ' Your argument is still yours (because remember that you are re-presenting learning) but you are now supporting it, which means that it becomes more valid.

Sometimes, also, when students are asked to be reflective and present their stance, they write what might be termed 'platitudes' – statements like: 'I strongly believe that all children should be equal and, therefore, I want my research to impact on the inclusion practice in my school'. In what way is this going to convince any reader that your belief is really yours and distinctly so? There is no doubt that all educators want equality and inclusion to be central to all practice, unless they have gone into teaching with ulterior psychopathic motives. The statement, therefore, becomes a 'platitude'. What about saying instead that 'because all children are expected to be treated equally by law, education is, *as so and so has stated*, a complex and challenging field of practice'. In the latter statement, you are acknowledging your knowledge of the law and your evidence from the literature that things are not always simple to tackle on the ground. You have a law, on the one hand, and then you have a set of practices, on the other, which you want to improve. Your belief is not necessarily about 'all children should be treated equally' (that is a given and is the law of the land), but rather about the 'so what' of the linkages between values, regulations, law and the practice on the ground. Your argument is really about how you need to have a positive impact on educational practice. Academic readers are not interested in givens, but rather in how these givens can be tackled more effectively in practice and linked to thinking or re-thinking what is already out there. Readers also need to learn about new stuff, new thinking, and you are giving them that by shining your lamp on new aspects of theorising from your integrative perspective (Drawing 5.1).

DRAWING 5.1   Re-present machine

How to define and structure a research enquiry

The first thing to do with any piece of work or research is to label it or define it. Both research designs and ethical approval applications, as well as specific professional practice assignments (such as, for example, reports or case studies), are much better framed if given relevant titles. The key terms of the **title or definition** need to be explicitly explained. What is the definition of 'multilingual', for instance? Is it going to be the dictionary definition or the more moderated (less categorical) ones that exist in the literature? At postgraduate level, one is asked to use more of the literature around and more evaluated and proven definitions. The dictionary definition for 'multilingual' is someone who speaks many languages fluently. However, in terms of education, multilingual also means one who is exposed to more than two languages and, even if they do not speak both these languages, they may be deemed multilingual.

That is because the literature definition is about recognising the importance of language as being part of identity and everyday experience rather than just a matter of proficiency. In addition, in terms of education, a multilingual person may well be someone who will require extra support with acquiring English as an additional language.

The literature recognises the many levels at which key terms can be understood. That is why each piece of work at postgraduate level needs to be defined and properly structured. It needs to highlight very clearly and very precisely what key aspects of the issue being defined and researched are now going to be scrutinised and explained further. For example, with multilingualism being defined as pertaining to someone who is exposed to more than two languages, it may well then be worth **contextualising** further by looking at who multilinguals are, and how they may be distributed in, for example, a given context such as a school. In addition, there may be reliable statistics about the distribution of multilingualism within the country or its regions or individual schools. Again, it is all up to you to build your structure around the main definition or title that you have chosen to study further. For instance, if you are not concerned with recruitment of multilingual students in schools, then you may opt not to have sections tackling that within your writing. However, if your focus is more about the achievement of multilingual students in secondary schools, at a specific stage and for a few chosen subjects, then you may want to contextualise further by identifying key figures relating to that specific context. This precision in defining your enquiry or, if you prefer, focusing it, allows you then to structure your writing in a more cohesive and convincing way. You can be said to have now 'positioned' your enquiry. This is also considered an important aspect of criticality. At postgraduate level, the writer needs to be explicit as to where they are coming from, as well as their sources (Student Example 5.2). More than that, postgraduate-level writers need to treat some of their sources with scepticism (not quite cynically, but symptomatically) and ask themselves such questions as: 'Why would he say that?' and 'Does this author have an axe to grind?'

Student example 5.2   Integrity as a piece of writing

Theresa is writing a 3500-word case study of two learners with differing learning needs as an assignment to address a module on Special Educational Needs and Disabilities (SEND) at postgraduate level. She forgets to write a title and to define exactly what aspects of SEND she has decided to look at. In the first 1000 words, she covers many aspects of the literature on SEND and we are still uncertain about which specific definition of SEND she is espousing as well as what the parameters of the study are. Indeed, there has not been a definition of what SEND means, nor of whether the focus is on learning, teaching, assessment, achievement or any other aspects of education that are in need of being examined and why. The essay feels vague and does not guide the reader straight through the body of work that they are supposed to be focusing on. In that sense, the criticality is absent because there is not precision in terms of what the thinking behind **key terms** is about and why. The focus is not contextualised either. This piece of writing fails, not so much on the grounds of being badly written but, more importantly, on the grounds of being vague and unable to justify its own existence, because it has no integrity as a piece of writing on its own merit.

Student Example 5.2 highlights the value of having a structure for all academic writing. The following model essay plan can be adapted for most types of written assignments:

- *Title*: May be given by the course, but, if not, make it short and to the point.
- *Introduction*: Clearly define the precise aspect of the topic you are investigating.
- *Summary of central argument*: What will you claim and what evidence will you bring?
- *Context*: Political, economic, social, organisational.
- *Five or six key points*: Try to present evidence that supports and challenges.
- *Analysis*: You are making judgements about the evidence for and against.
- *Conclusion*: Draws together the core argument and its implications.
- *References*: Take care to use correct referencing style.

How to pursue an effective argument

In the previous section, we concluded that a piece of writing at postgraduate level needs to have integrity and to be in a position to stand on its own merit. This is also highly dependent on the effectiveness of the central argument being made. If writing, at any level, not just at postgraduate level, lacks a central argument that helps the text cohere and hang together, it becomes useless. Markers or readers also mention the 'woolliness' of some arguments. This latter criticism is about arguments that might have a good premise but are not developed and explained very well. 'Woolliness' could also mean giving too much detail that is descriptive, not analytical and not relating to the main argument.

Postgraduate-level writing is about demonstrating an explicit and convincing structured development of an argument. This kind of writing shows extremely strong internal consistency (question, premises, evidence, conclusions). It will make the work convincingly holistic. In addition, excellent postgraduate-level writing always shows evidence of a creative and original approach, with a critical awareness of its strengths and limitations. Indeed, the best dissertations, for example, are very clear and explicit about their own **critical stance**, with evidence of where their ideas come from and explicit explanations and analyses of how the author will go about supporting (or challenging) argument/s through evidence-based research that is robust, ethical, well developed and structured. Everything that is written, including the concluding remarks and future recommendations, needs to be going back to the initial central argument and whether the question is answered fully or not and why.

Each section of a dissertation or essay addresses aspects of the argument or its premises. Given that we are tackling academic writing at postgraduate level, it is worth remembering that an **academic argument** is an evidence-based defence of a non-obvious position on a complex issue. Unlike a personal essay, which can rely on personal experience and general observations, a research paper must draw on evidence – usually in the form of direct quotations or statistics from peer-reviewed academic journals. If we go back to the example of the SEND Student Example 5.2 tackled in the previous section, it is really about finding the central argument about which premise of SEND the author wants to talk about and gather evidence to support or challenge this. SEND, like any other area of education, is a complex issue and one might defend aspects of it based on research, but not necessarily on commonly held assumptions. There are assumptions (based also on robust research, guidance and policies) that 'reasonable adjustments' can really support learners to achieve. However, you might be interested in wanting to argue that such adjustments sometimes hinder achievement. As an academic argument, this might be deemed to be controversial, but it is perfectly valid if you have evidence to support this and sway your audience to your own way of thinking in a coherent, purposeful and well-structured way (Student Example 5.3).

Student example 5.3   Linking the methods to the methodology

Zak has failed his dissertation because he did not write his rationale and concluding discussion in terms of what the research was about and what the main thesis, argument and evidence were about. The work felt disjointed and the readers mentioned the need for him to go over every chapter and section of the dissertation relating all aspects to the main argument that he is exploring; he should be asking a question as opposed to trying to prove a point. For instance, in a methodology chapter, he does not relate back to the need to have certain methods for gathering and analysing data, as against others. Indeed, there does not seem to be any justification for the choice of methods and no explicit relation is made between methodology and what he is trying to illuminate. For example, why have a quantitative questionnaire and statistical analysis if he is trying to gauge the voice of those who are the key participants in a qualitative study?

As we have pointed out elsewhere (see especially the sections in Chapter 1 on 'Scaffolding and Mind Maps' and 'Resilience and Perseverance', and the sub-section in Chapter 6 on 'Postgraduate Assignment'), more attention to the assessment criteria relevant to his studies could have put Zak onto a more productive pathway.

How to convince audiences

The way to convince audiences is to be very explicit, clear and have solid evidence to make your point acceptable. Academic work is about being very well informed and not being categorical about results unless you have an extreme wealth of good-quality evidence that cannot easily be refuted. Most academic work remains like a body of knowledge that one adds to by augmenting the evidence base or by redefining the earlier premises or parameters of previous research. The best way to **write for an audience** is to be very explicit about what you are writing about or researching, how you will go about supporting it and why this is important. Then, when you have actually given the evidence, which is very often in the form of data results and interpretation that are reliable and coherent, your conclusions are reached in the most compelling way. That is why at the top grade of postgraduatelevel writing, one of the key criteria is that the author has demonstrated **explicit and convincing structured development**. Bear in mind here that the key criteria are about being very clear or explicit, as well as being very well structured and convincing in how the whole piece of work is developed. The important thing here is to remember that you are writing for an audience or reader, and not for yourself.

Knowing your audience is very important, whether you are writing or presenting orally. For postgraduate-level academic work, your audience is part of a community of practice that will need highly cogent and very well-developed arguments that can win them over. It is very important that you write or speak with this audience in mind. What seems evident to you may not be so to others, unless you have explicitly explained what you are doing and clearly supported your findings so that your argument is made at the end. There are many tips for doing that effectively, but one of the most useful approaches is to have **critical readers** who can tell you whether everything that you have written makes sense to them. They are your 'mock' audience and can help you review your work so that everything is made crystal clear to those you are writing for. Academic work is a shared enterprise in this sense, as well as in how it informs others about new ideas and developments in knowledge and practice.

In addition, if you want to convince anyone, it has to start with yourself and so the advice is never to submit work at postgraduate level unless you, as its author, are completely satisfied that it has integrity and has the power to convince those who receive it – even if it is to conclude that there is no one definitive 'answer'.

With orally presented work, you will also need to rehearse in front of a 'mock' audience and note down their feedback, acting on it as much as you can so as to enhance your final presentation. You can also record yourself speaking and check how clearly presented your arguments and your evidence are by playing the recording back and noting down areas for development for yourself. Do also watch good lectures or speeches, such as the TED online lectures, which are master classes of excellent structure, clarity, evidence and knowledgeably presented arguments and theses. In general, try to listen to as many very well-crafted live talks or lectures in any area that you appreciate, such as on History, Art or Science. With writing, try and read well-written and peer-reviewed articles in academic journals related to the area/s that you are interested in researching. The more you read good-quality academic texts, the more you are likely to become a better academic writer. The embedding of good written or oral practice comes from being actively receptive to the skills of reading and listening.

Student example 5.4   The core of the academic argument

Abeyomi has submitted a draft extended essay for a module at postgraduate level about 'Authentic and Effective Leadership in Working with Families and Children'. His tutor has commented on the draft and said that his 'thesis' is unclear. Abeyomi is unsure what 'thesis' means in this context, as the tutor is clearly not talking about a thesis in the sense of a whole dissertation. The personal tutor explains that, in this case, a 'thesis' is a sentence or two that presents the author's opinion about the topic: it is the core of the **academic argument**. Abeyomi is reminded about how it is important to write with convincing explicitness that 'grabs' one's reader from the start. The tutor says:

> A good thesis clarifies or explains why you hold this opinion (regardless of whether I agree with it or not, but so long as it can be evidenced through the literature and reliable data). A good persuasive essay has a strong thesis that gives the essay unity. The best way to do that is to avoid ambiguity and vagueness; for example: 'I think that maybe the government should fund leadership courses.' A stronger thesis would be: 'The government should fund multi-professional leadership because … [provide reasons here]).'

The tutorial in Student Example 5.4 suggests that the tutor is urging Abeyomi to work on the opening of his essay and make his opinion very explicit from the start, not shying away from putting forward a well-evidenced thesis that can be defended in the rest of the essay. This would be done via many arguments such as: the inclusion of many more hard-to-reach families who are needed for gauging the voice of diverse stakeholders; or the need for children and family services to remain part of the national debate on educational leadership standards; or any other argument that he may want to put forward. He is advised to provide a range of evidence for each argument that challenges or supports it, to show thoughtfulness, balance, reflection and criticality.

How to research and use key terms

One way of starting on the path of your research, and then writing or presenting your ideas, is to pay close attention to key words or terms. These will enable you to carry out enlightening literature searches, as well as to narrow down your work to key aspects that illuminate or identify your research. At the start of any research project at postgraduate level, be it for an essay or for a dissertation, you can simply type into your computer the terms that define your interest or concern. As a postgraduate student, you also have access to your academic library search engines, which operate in a similar way to Google. For example, if you are interested in researching the field of community health and in particular the contribution of health psychologists, you can start with the following terms as your basis: 'community health'; 'health psychologist'. As you narrow down your field of study, you may want to further delineate these terms. For example, it may well be that you are interested in the impact of 'health intervention projects' on 'community behaviour change'. Remember that the inverted commas tell the search engine that it is the whole phrase that you are interested in, not the component words.

As you research your identified key terms, you will come across a substantial body of research in the form of academic articles and books, as well as a wealth of policy documents, reports and case studies from the grey literature. This initial search and reading may even help you change your research focus and be more certain about what exactly you want to research. If you are a health practitioner, you may well be interested in enhancing your own department's policies and practice, and the literature search is likely to put you in touch with good practice on this topic from other departments or from well-developed research projects that have used reliable methodologies. This, in itself, might stimulate you to read more about the kind of methodologies that others have used and start designing your own way of how to collect, interpret and analyse data. As you research at this initial stage through reading and reflecting, you are, in effect, starting to formulate a research project of your own, weighing the pros and cons of particular methods for dealing with data and gaining knowledge on what works (or does not work) in research. You can then relate this to your own setting and see how aspects from the literature can be adapted to your own professional context.

How to start on the research path and formulate a high-level research question which is good enough for you to be in a position to answer it, within a given timeframe and with adequate methods, may be likened to the metaphor of focusing your camera lens from '**the forest to the leaf**'.

The forest is your overall interest or concern, such as, for example, childhood obesity. The tree then becomes the primary schooling phase, for instance. The branch could be defined as pupils aged around 7 years, or at Key Stage 1. The leaf could then be the urban community school type (or a context outside of school, such as, for example, lower-income families). This example of a metaphor shows you how you could develop this whole discovery into a research question, such as: 'How does childhood obesity affect the learning of pupils aged 7 years in an urban community school?' or 'How does childhood obesity affect the well-being of children from lower-income families?'

As you research the key terms of 'childhood obesity', 'primary school child(ren)' and 'urban community schools' or 'early childhood' and 'lower-income families', you will be able to see what literature already exists on these topics. On the other hand, you may have started with just throwing in key terms such as: 'childhood obesity', 'primary schools' and 'urban community schools', 'early childhood', 'lower-income families', and ended up with one of the two research questions mentioned above. The trajectory need not always be one where you are certain as you go about narrowing down your forest to your leaf. The metaphor helps you either way. It can help you propose a **high-level research question** or it can also support your initial ideas and discover what can be done for your research later.

Academic integration

As a postgraduate student, you may not feel as supported as you did as an undergraduate student. In addition, you may have work, family and other commitments which will prevent you from being always able to integrate socially in the university in the manner that a first-year undergraduate and younger student would do. In that sense, your goal is not necessarily about social integration, such as making friends or personal contact with academic staff. Your primary goal is to achieve a PGCert or Master's or EdD, including various modules and a dissertation at the end or a PhD by thesis. You are a strongly independent learner who needs to focus on academic integration more than anything else at this stage of your trajectory. Academic integration is also about commitment and being goal-orientated.

The best way to enhance your own academic integration is to conduct yourself as a true independent learner. This means reading, actively engaging with the resources posted on your VLE, and participating in seminars and lectures, including online activities. Also helpful will be blogging and

VLE posting with other postgraduate students on your course. Your work will be nourished and enhanced if you can create and maintain a network of like-minded independent students who not only support you but also stimulate you towards an ongoing commitment to achieving at postgraduate level. You will also need to be very familiar with the grading system and assessment criteria for your course and with how to use feedback from tutors to improve your work. Those students who try and meet their academic tutor at least once per module, and their supervisor many times and regularly, whilst in the process of doing their dissertations, have found themselves more academically rewarded and more able to integrate all the skills needed to become an achieving postgraduate student. These meetings can also be made electronically and being a distance student should not deter you from being in touch regularly with those who can support you and who know your work.

Academic integration is also about doing some personal development for yourself, setting targets and meeting them by planning what other skills you may need and reading as much around your different ideas as possible. Extra reading is key so that you can get immersed in the academic way of presenting and writing and, in turn, increase your own academic self-esteem. Ask yourself: 'Am I doing well academically?' and if you are in any doubt, read books that guide you towards enhancing your skills, attend as many seminars as you can, review and use the resources (including those about study skills) that your academic library recommends and, finally, but most importantly, talk to your tutors or supervisors. Academic staff are always very happy to listen to students talk about their own learning and give guidance for any developments that they want to undertake. Thinking and speaking about your own learning can, in fact, further prove to yourself and to others involved in your development that you are academically integrated and able to think in a meta-cognitive way about learning. Academic integration is also part of the enjoyment of the subjects that you have chosen to study, including the study patterns and the requirements made by the course. It is when you get into the immersion of reading, researching and addressing the requirements of your various modules that you feel more fulfilled and able to transfer knowledge and experience from one area of your study to another.

Finally, academic integration is also about identifying with the academic practice within the course and university, as well as within the literature that you read and research. At the university, it is about identifying with academic norms and values, such as ethics, reliable sources of information and, as a student, with processes and procedures that enhance your experience, such as course management committees, feedback to your tutor about your experience on a course or a module and making the most of your role as a student who can also be a driver of quality in academic practice at your own university (Student Example 5.5).

Student example 5.5   Taking part

Hannah was at risk of withdrawing from her course and was not progressing as well as she would have liked to. A chance meeting with one of her module tutors made her realise that she had not engaged at all with any of the many course materials posted on the VLE, to the extent that she did not even know the number of credits that she needed to gather in order to pass her Master's. She lacked self-esteem because her grades had not been good enough and she had many reassessments to submit her first year of study. She had not looked at any of the extra reading posted online, nor had she replied to the posts that were regularly placed by other students on her course who were all involved in some form of peer learning and of reviewing each other's ideas and drafts. She had also missed out on what the library and student services were offering in terms of study skills guidance and search engines to support her modules.

It is only after talking it over with one tutor that she realised that she had many entitlements as a postgraduate student that she had not used profitably for herself, such as the right to a minimum of one tutorial for each module and that some tutors could also help her with formative feedback on her early assignment drafts. Once she started integrating herself into the academic practice of her specific university, and entering into a dialogue about academic norms and values, including those that apply to independent learning and to student support, she then started developing herself and enhanced her skills and started progressing more rapidly.

The key question you need to ask yourself is 'Am I enjoying myself at the university?' – and try and do something about your own experience if you are not. You are responsible for your own learning and need to be proactive in making it better for yourself and for achieving the best outcomes that you can.

Key ideas and terms

Representation of learning or shining a new lamp on ideas and adding your perspective.

Dialogue or entering into a discourse beyond the initial perceived experience or idea.

Reflective 'I' that believes in being informed, not merely opinioned or subject to platitudes.

Theorising, or re-theorising what is already out there, by giving new life to various ideas via a process of evaluation, analysis and integration.

Title or definition of a key piece of writing at postgraduate level, such as a case study assignment, a research enquiry, a design for a research project or ethics application, needs to be seeped in research literature so that you have a more 'moderated' and realistic overall topic.

Contextualisation is key, so as to focus your writing or your research design and so that the parameters of its scope are precise and convincing.

Key terms, or being very clear about your parameters and what frames your overall argument, are very important. It is crucial to define them in a 'moderated' researched way, not using mundane dictionary definitions. The latter tend to be categorical and do not necessarily allow for the relativism of real terms in real contexts.

Critical stance is also about being explicit concerning where you are coming from and where your sources are from, too. This is about situating yourself and your sources, or further contextualising in a responsible manner.

Internal consistency of an argument, or a series of interrelated arguments, is what makes a text coherent and holistic, so that everything hangs together very clearly and relates back to the main thesis or argument.

Academic argument is different to any other argument as it often means tackling issues that are far less obvious than we think, or even countering the commonly held trends. Academic arguments need solid evidence and premises that are very clearly and explicitly articulated.

Arguments, premises and theses are very important in order to enhance the quality of any piece of postgraduate-level writing or presentation. If, as an example, an argument is about how some types of reasonable adjustments are not always useful for maximising achievement, then the premise is that the author is interested in the impact of SEND adjustments on achievement and therefore everything must rally around this main thesis, including evidence, theorising, methodology and discussion, so as to try and defend this main argument.

Writing for an audience. This is likely to be the most important reason why academic writing (or speaking) is a shared enterprise that is part of a set of conventions where the way in which you present has to be very well constructed, convincing and evidenced in a robust manner.

Explicit and convincing structured development is very important to bear in mind in all aspects of postgraduate-level work. Never assume that your audience will guess what you want to describe, analyse and prove, unless you have explicitly addressed the needs of your readers or listeners and paid attention to the very highly structured development of your thesis.

Critical readers are one of the most important people who can help you tighten up your academic postgraduate-level writing and tell you which areas need improving. You can also have critical listeners who would be those people helping you as you rehearse a speech or a paper.

Forest to leaf is a metaphor that you may find useful when sifting through all of your ideas of what, how and why to research. You work yourself through, further delineating your key terms and contextualising them as clearly as possible.

High-level research question is when your research focus is such that all of your key terms are known and very clearly identified in a way that will enable you to answer the question within a reasonable timescale and in a context-sensitive way, including your own setting or one that you aspire to work in.

Chapter summary

In this chapter, we have explored the skills and aptitudes necessary at postgraduate level. These encourage you to be independent, convincing, well researched, well structured, well integrated and able to achieve your goals as best you can. The chapter prepares the ground for the more practical, hands-on skills of writing and presenting orally of Chapter 6. The chapter very much engages you to be a thinker not only about your own work, but also about the work of others. It reminds you that you are theorising, analysing, reflecting and actively arguing in a clear reader-centred (or listener-centred) style. You are the person who is responsible for your own development, even more so at postgraduate level, than at any other level of study before that. Your confidence with postgraduate-level work will only grow and reward you with achievement, if you fully realise the importance of your place within an academic community of practice, where explicit, unambiguous, well-argued theses are highly valued.

6

The Postgraduate-Level Linguistic Skills

Chapter overview

This chapter delves into the very practical aspects of writing and presenting academic work. It starts with a look at the linguistic traits of postgraduate-level work and takes the reader through the nature of academic language as a specialised discourse that exists alongside many others. It tries to demystify for the student the perceived complexity of the deep nature of this **discourse** by likening it to acquiring a new language, or at least a new variety of this language. The focus of the chapter is therefore about equipping the student with the confidence to pursue the goal of becoming skilled at academic discourse. The intention is not an instrumentalist one. It is not about churning out correct grammar and vocabulary, on which there are numerous online resources and courses (including those offered at any decent student services department in any university) which can help students distinguish their adverbs from their adjectives, as well as use the right link words between their paragraphs, and all sorts of other techniques for writing correct texts.

The intention of this chapter is primarily to treat academic language more in a reflective and enjoyable way that comes from a critical understanding of what this discourse is all about, how to become comfortable with it and why it is of critical importance for success in any outputs at postgraduate level. The chapter and its examples stress the importance of being engaged with developing the main features of this discourse so that postgraduate-level criteria are met. There is a look at the functions and skills of language in general and then a mapping of those that pertain only to academic modes of writing and speaking, such as 'synthesising' and 'stating'.

The chapter also emphasises the role of the audience, writing for a reader and speaking for a listener. It finishes with a look at English for academic purposes (EAP), which should be of benefit to international and home students alike, once again considering the main common features of academic discourse.

The linguistic skills needed at postgraduate level

Knowing that there are differences in writing or speaking systems and in levels of literacy or oracy is very important to anyone progressing from undergraduate to postgraduate study, or returning to education and embarking on postgraduate study after a long time spent working. The main basic linguistic skills of any language are the writing, reading, speaking and listening ones. But underneath (and governing) these basic skills there are rules and systems of **pragmatics, semantics and syntax** that may change the way in which the four basic skills are promoted to the surface of everyday speech or writing by any given member of a speech community.

To say, 'I wonder if you could ...,' for example, is a form of **hedging** that is employed in English with the intention of requesting, or even politely ordering something from someone, as in the statement: 'I wonder if you could close the window.' This is probably conceived by some speakers to be better than saying the more straightforward 'Close the window!' because, in certain circumstances, the intention is to be hedging towards what one wants and hence to be appearing polite. The conditional form 'if you could', therefore, addresses the functionality of a polite request or order and not merely that of a dream-like condition such as 'If I were a rich man ...' and, consequently, grammar alone cannot explain the best way in which the language is used (because a conditional form in any English grammar book is not naturally associated with polite requests). This is why English is best learned as **a functional system** of rules and common understandings that implies that grammar and lexis are used expertly to convey a multitude of meanings and intentions. The deeper pragmatic, syntactic and semantic components of language kick in and transform the basic skills of writing and speaking into expert tools for conveying complex and inspiring ideas intentionally. Incidentally, hedging is used rather liberally in academic language to avoid being dogmatic about the knowledge and information that we want to put forward.

In formal academic writing or speaking in the Humanities and Social Sciences, there is a set of overarching **meta-functions** that are important and these include reporting, reflecting, criticising, analysing, synthesising, arguing, introducing and concluding, among many other formal intentions of writing or speaking within the discourse of academia. We call these 'meta-functions' here because they are also the key criteria by which your work will be judged. They are so engrained in academic language use that they become almost like skills rather than mere intentions pertaining to the author and his or her texts. Even though academic language seems to be stating the 'what' of an argument, on the surface, it is ultimately always trying to do so with depth of analysis, critique, reflection and synthesis. In that sense, it needs to be tightly drafted and very explicit.

Academic English is thus a highly specialised discourse that is best understood as a distinctive style, different and separated from everyday English. If you think of it as a language variety with its own conventions and rules, you are more likely to understand the need to become a highly proficient user of it. This is probably why international students who are already fluent in everyday English can become experts at it, just like home students who are native speakers of English, because, regardless of how much English you know, you still need to 'acquire' academic English, a distinctive English variety with its own rules and conventions. One could argue that whether you are a native speaker or not is irrelevant to the process of acquisition and, in that sense, all students should begin on an equal footing. In some cases, international students have more academic support (and, indeed, should maximise such support to the extent that they can), such as pre-sessional courses in aspects of highly specialised academic English, and that may put them at an advantage, particularly if they have already developed high levels of formal English in previous study, or, indeed, have learned their native language at a very advanced academic level, prior to embarking on English-medium study. Whatever the circumstances, the skills of academic writing and speaking need to be honed and considered to be similar to acquiring a new language for a specific purpose (hence **English for academic purposes** or EAP).

The skills needed at postgraduate level pertain to this skilful use of language in order to convey accurately the functions of text and the intentions of the author. One of the key linguistic skills is to have the correct lexis or, if you like, the relevant 'vocabulary or terminology'. By reading academic articles and books in your field as well as attending conferences where papers on your subject or allied to it are being presented, you will undeniably enhance the **nomenclature** (set of words and names) that is relevant to your subject. For example, within the nomenclature of Sociology, one will understand the meaning of the word 'habitus' and how to use it, and this will be different from how the term is specifically understood and used in other allied fields, such as in Education Studies, Literary Studies or Health.

Postgraduate students are advised to purchase specialist dictionaries or acquire glossaries of terms used in their own subjects, with examples of contextual usage so as to facilitate their full acquisition. Indeed, it is really important to be an expert in one's field and to use the relevant vocabulary with ease. It is this high level of precise and expert knowledge of the key terms behind your work that distinguishes you as a postgraduate from any other higher education student (Student Example 6.1).

Student example 6.1 Make use of specialised nomenclature

Let us examine a statement written by Adana for an essay on bilingual education at postgraduate level:

> We think that the old way of having power over the language that pupils speak at school and how they are judged on that by allowing them to speak only English is not useful anymore. The society has changed and not everyone speaks only English in some areas.

She has expressed her thinking about the topic in general terms, which make no use of the specialised nomenclature of Education Studies. After a tutorial and feedback on the early draft of the essay, Adana transforms the statement into a more specialised sentence, in which, you will note, many terms have become tighter and more relevant to the academic discipline of Education Studies required for this topic. The terms that we consider to be specialised and pertaining to educational policy, bilingualism and professional practice are in italic in order to illustrate the expertise of the author:

> The research argues that archaic, *centralised, monolingual curriculum and assessment policies* do not seem to be *fit for purpose* for an increasingly *diverse* population, especially in *classrooms* where *English native speakers* may, indeed, be in a *minority*.

You will also note that the transformed sentence has synthesised Adana's critical ideas of power and unilateral decision-making relating to past educational school policies into a more polished text. It does that by arguing more precisely that the (now *archaic* – in itself an interesting word as it prefigures the student's critical stance) system was too *centralised* and *monolingual* in the way in which it imposed *curriculum and assessment policies* on school populations. It is also interesting that the phrase '*fit for purpose*' strikes more firmly at the heart of the argument about diversity of school populations and flexibility within curricula and assessment than the weaker, and rather woolly, '*useful*' in the earlier draft of the sentence.

You might argue that this is all about jargon and being in with the in-crowd, impressing your audience (even showing off). Perhaps that is what it is all about at one level (that of professional pride), except that we would encourage you to keep working at it and enhancing the skills that will enable you to be part of an academic community that deeply respects precision, clarity and knowledge of the fields of enquiry, including how best to convey ideas and arguments via well-balanced texts that speak directly to it. The aim is to produce a sophisticated, professional and eloquent text that is as close as possible to a publishable standard.

Writing and polishing academic texts

To ensure that you have an eloquent text that makes sense to your audience, you would need to draft and redraft, polishing every single word, sentence and paragraph to create a coherent whole that reads fluently and accurately. Polishing and reviewing your writing is key (Drawing 6.1). One way of checking is to see whether your punctuation is correct and that your sentences are well constructed. You can do this by giving your text to someone else to read and asking them to highlight areas where they do not quite understand clearly what your message is. This will be one way of knowing whether you

DRAWING 6.1   Final final final *draft*

are meeting the key criterion of clarity. Without clarity, you lose the impact on your audience. Also, the more you write and read, the more your skills improve and the more it becomes easier for you to produce well-constructed texts. The best writers take time developing the finished product and are known to produce at least five drafts of the final piece of writing. Do not worry about individual words in your first draft and instead concentrate on putting your ideas, arguments and knowledge on paper. That first draft is really more like a plan than a finished product. Train yourself to explain the detail later and then finesse your words and stylistic features such as grammar and punctuation thereafter. As you finally review your work, you will see exactly where the improvements should be made. At the end, when you feel satisfied with what you have written, share your output with a critical friend who will be in a position to tell you whether what you have written makes sense. You must always remember that you are writing for a reader, not for yourself.

Some students think that producing long sentences with very complex grammar and somewhat pompous words is what makes their style academic. It is the reverse that is conducive to comprehension. Indeed, simple grammar with well-chosen words and clarity of expression are the ingredients of good academic writing. Being aware of jargon and detailing meanings to your readers in plain, accessible language is also very important because only you know what you are trying to say about your subject and need to appreciate its deeper semantics. Your task is to eliminate confusion and explain everything that is technical or highly specialised to your audience. This is why students are often asked to identify their key words and address their exact meaning systematically. This also applies to all acronyms, which must be completely spelled out when used for the first time in a text and even explained. For example, using the acronym NICE, without first spelling out that the letters denote the National Institute for Health and Care Excellence and explaining succinctly what NICE's remit is, can exclude, rather than include, your diverse audiences. Remember that not all your readers would be familiar with the way in which healthcare is organised in England. It is important to never assume that what you know is also necessarily known by your audience.

Often students ask whether they should use the first or third person when writing. At least in the subject areas of Education, Health and Professional Studies, we would recommend that you use the reflective 'I', and that means being direct and using the first person but making sure that it is supported by evidence (see the section in Chapter 5 on 'Positionality and the Reflective "I"'). It is considered ugly to write in the third person when actually meaning the first person. Phrases like 'the present author wishes to ...' are much better expressed instead as 'I wish to ...' as it is preferable not to spend so many redundant words saying something which, after all, is not what you genuinely mean. That is why the phrase 'the author wishes ...' might appear ugly (or clunky) rather than clear, genuine and to the point.

Even though literacy is not a sufficient condition for postgraduate-level achievement, it is, nevertheless, a necessary requirement in all the minds of those who will be reading your work. Remember that you are addressing an academic community (as was explained in Chapter 5) and that your writing has a very specialised purpose. At its most basic level, your work must be absolutely free of spelling mistakes, of grammatical solecisms (for example, sentences without verbs), of confusing punctuation (or the absence of punctuation when it is needed to help a reader make sense of what you are saying), and with no misused words (malapropisms). Academic writing must remain literal, to the point, as to write obscurely harms your intention of having the desired positive impact on your audience and of obtaining high grades.

There is an aspect of academic English writing that is to do with precision whilst being judicious with the word count. Academic English uses what are called 'premodifiers'. These are words that modify your main terms in order to economise on redundant words and get straight to the point in a tidy way (Student Example 6.2).

Student example 6.2   Premodifiers: In a nutshell

Take, for instance, the following statement in Nadim's essay: 'This focus on the nature of language taking a cognitive solution is one of great significance.' If Nadim were to change this statement to: 'A cognitive approach to language is highly significant,' not only will he be economising eight words, but he will also be far clearer as to his intentions. The key term, 'approach to language', is premodified by the addition of the word 'cognitive', which, in a nutshell, tells us exactly what he is stating rather than waiting for the longer phrase of 'taking a cognitive solution', which makes the earlier sentence less precise and a lot longer.

This economy with language and precision with your words comes from polishing drafts until they appear crystal clear to you and your reader/s.

Another grammatical feature of academic English is called 'nominalisation'. This is when you make something sound like a noun when, in reality, it is not. For example, 'The National Health Service (NHS) is in danger of ...,' is a nominalisation as, in reality, the NHS is not a human being but an abstract noun that is not capable of putting itself in danger. However, you spend less time skirting the issue by nominalising abstract words, especially if they are key to your argument. The thing is to then go into the detail of why you think that the NHS is in danger and then, perhaps, explain who the actors could be, if you have to. In that sense, nominalisations are helpful in making you get straight to the point. Occasionally, students spend too many words introducing an essay by saying things like, 'In this essay, I shall try and …,' rather than nominalising and going straight to the point by saying, 'This essay will …' It is perfectly logical that the essay becomes almost like an actor and therefore can become the subject of your opening sentence. It is assumed that you are the agent behind this essay and everyone knows that when they read it.

Planning and presenting work orally

When you are planning to present your work orally, you must remember to prepare just as thoroughly as when you are writing. In some ways, it is even harder to present orally than it is to write because you have to be doubly suc-cinct and find ways in which to engage your audience through voice, body language, eye contact and well-worked out visual and/or audio material. The key is to rehearse your presentation and to think of your audience all the time. At the forefront of your thinking must also be the quality of your con-tent, which has to be engaging and inspiring. Any topic can be made to be enjoyable and you must find ways to introduce the support of aids like PowerPoint presentations that are well sequenced, with clear, short text and, if relevant, punctuated by interesting images or even short films.

Drawing up a plan of what you need to cover will help you formulate aims and objectives for your presentation. Why are you presenting the content (your aims) and what do you expect your audience to get from it (your objec-tives), are key components of your talk. When planning your introduction, think of a 'hook' that you can present to engage your audience from the start. Good orators are always inspiring in how they engage their audience and perhaps use humour or images to set the context of their talk. The structure is very important, too, in that there must be a good flow between the different aspects of your presentation. Signposting with phrases like, 'I will demon-strate next what I mean by …,' or words that list the different phases of an argument, like 'first, second, third …', can help listeners access the meaning more easily and meet the objectives that you have set for your presentation. In a PowerPoint presentation, you can also repeat key slides to bring the audience back to your objectives and to consolidate learning of the material that you are presenting.

Just like in writing, you need to make sure that there is a clarity and struc-ture to what you present. The difference with oral presentation is that you need to arrange and punctuate your material in a more visual and engaging and often very succinct way, leaving you with the chance to talk about the detail whilst your slides are summarising your key ideas. Spoken punctuation is also about having the right level of eye contact, which is inclusive and shows that your audience is the most important aspect of your talk. Other punctuating devices include some amount of repetition, rephrasing and rhetoric so that people remember what you are saying and have a chance to consolidate the knowledge that they are gaining from your talk. As you reach the end of your talk, you need to go over the material once again, summarising the key points that have been covered and linking back to the start of your presentation so as to show how you have addressed the aims and objectives that you set out for your audience.

Just like in writing for a reader, you speak for a listener and need to remind yourself that listening to a talk is an ephemeral activity where information is not easily retained, unless the speaker has planned meticulously well for how to engage his or her audience fully. In that sense, presenting by reading long texts from slides or from notes is not at all conducive to engaging your audience. You would need to rehearse speaking the material (rather than reading) and making eye contact with your audience whilst showing a high level of preparation in the visual material that you show via PowerPoint, Prezi or other means for communicating complex academic content. During practice of your presentation, you will be in a position to refine your script and perhaps highlight phrases and key words that you need to remember or emphasise.

Some students like to use sketches or diagrams to remind themselves of the structure, with key content to go with it. This technique will stop you from reading and give you more confidence when speaking about your content. It is also very important to know your specialist subject vocabulary, both in terms of what it means and how to pronounce and spell it, as well as being meticulous about the referencing and citing of your academic sources. Just as you would produce many redrafts of a finished essay or dissertation, the point is to remember that spoken material will also need to be honed through a few rehearsals and redrafts of the final script and its visual summary.

You could also introduce literary devices such as figures of speech or rhetoric, which is the study of the art of discourse for purposes of engaging and persuading audiences. Literary devices can be effective, if only to pose a problem, for example at the start of your presentation, or to encourage imagination and open up the floor to questions and discussion. It is therefore worth listening to good lectures and talks and to note down the devices used by good speakers, such as repetition, rhetorical questions and metaphors (Student Example 6.3).

Student example 6.3   Presentation format

If you are new to giving presentations, you would need a tried-and-trusted formula. Ask about examples from past papers and look at the structure and content expected for an oral assignment. One such format or formula is as follows and it can be adapted for Professional Studies, Health and Education:

- Introduction/overview/hook
- Theoretical framework/research questions/problem-posing
- Methodology/case selection/sampling/ethical issues
- Literature review
- Discussion of data/findings
- Analysis
- Conclusion

Different discourses for different audiences

Even though we spoke before about English for academic purposes (or EAP) as if it is a homogeneous discourse (see the section in this chapter on 'The Linguistic Skills Needed at Postgraduate Level'), there are differences within it (see the section below on EAP). In this section, we tackle the differences that pertain to the nature of the work and the specific audience that you are writing for or presenting to.

Postgraduate assignment

When you are writing an assignment for a specific module at Master's or doctoral level, you are addressing the module's intended learning outcomes and the assessment criteria that go with your level of study. The latter are always explicitly communicated to students through handbooks or module guides. In this scenario, your intended audience consists of a maximum of two markers (including almost always your module tutor) and, if necessary, one more experts to moderate (either internally or externally). These academics know the ins and outs of the module very well and have experience of marking at your level. It is therefore extremely important to have had some exposure to their way of seeing things and at the very least your module tutor's expectations of your work. Ask to have a tutorial in which you could test out your ideas or, if permissible, a formative draft of your finished assignment so that you engage with your tutor's style and expectations. Another aspect of writing for this kind of highly specialised and experienced audience is to look at past assignments, if available, and discuss with peers how they are all approaching the same assignment. The more you consciously think about and discuss your assignment, the more you will feel confident about how to write it. You are writing to gain a grade for your work and pass the module and this should be at the forefront of your hard work on this way of writing academically.

Presentation

When you are presenting your work orally, whether for a grade on a module or for a formative step towards a later written essay that will be marked, your audience will almost always consist of your peers, your tutors and occasionally also other members of the department. This can be a nerve-racking experience and so it is crucial that you prepare and practise meticulously. This kind of audience can be very intimidating because the perception of your peers and your tutors may appear to be quite judgemental and instant, as you will be in close proximity to them, noting their reactions to your material and style of delivery. Presenting to this kind of audience means being adept at delivering material confidently, clearly and succinctly and keeping to the time allocated.

Dissertation

When writing a dissertation (see Chapter 7), you need to remember that you are publishing your work to the wider academic public beyond your university. Indeed, a dissertation is a capstone piece of academic work that is a lot more detailed than an assignment. It will be arranged in chapters, with a table of contents, acknowledgements, an abstract, appendices and a substantial reference list. Even though the first readers of your dissertation may consist of only your tutor and a second academic expert, you need to remember that it can then be shared more widely and subsequently read by other students and academics at your university and elsewhere. The difficulty with writing for this kind of audience lies in recognising their expertise and therefore in being extra vigilant with your style, structure, coherence and robustness of argument. The way in which to think about it is that it must be seen as a first-step publication and, as such, must be of the highest possible standard.

Thesis

A doctoral thesis (see Chapter 7) is perhaps the most difficult piece of writing and the most scrutinised one that you may ever have to produce. The audience is large, very specialised and highly academic. It is also judged on its merits as a recognised contribution to knowledge. You enter the realm of the highest academic achievement when you pass your doctorate and this way of writing and presenting, therefore, has to be of the highest standard in all aspects. You will also be expected to present and explain your main findings in a viva voce examination (or oral examination, commonly known simply as a 'viva') to at least two experts in your field, who will have read your work and made notes, developing questions from this which they will use for a thorough discussion of your research with you. The challenges that you face with this kind of audience are those associated with expert knowledge and experience in research, publication, addressing others confidently and robust critical thinking. These kinds of personalities are only intimidating if you are unable to defend your thesis and prove to them how robust your research is. You need to have made sure that your thesis is extremely well crafted, convincing and thorough, with expert and critical analysis, synthesis and reflection.

Article

When you write an article (see the section in Chapter 8 on 'Getting Your Work Published'), which is sometimes an output during postgraduate study, you are probably accessing the highest, most prized writing and dissemination of research. This is because your work will be peer reviewed and scrutinised by a journal reviewer, who will ask you to make revisions if you are to be accepted as a contributor to the journal. Even for lesser-known journals, the stakes are high and you are very likely to be asked to make changes before the final publication. The writing is precise and quite succinct (as there are regulations on length, format and referencing which are published as 'Guidelines for Contributors'). The writing is targeted at the audience that the journal addresses and so it is important to see what kind of articles have already been published and therefore accepted, before proceeding to submit your writing Often, this means that you are contributing new knowledge or reporting on new data or ideas that will further the theoretical landscape relevant to your field. Some articles can be written in a rhetorical, provocative way, such as blogs or think pieces for specific organisations or websites. The main point with this kind of writing is to cover all key aspects of your research in a summarised but convincing manner and to polish your abstract, your key words, your introduction and your concluding remarks, making reference to recent literature and perhaps looking at international comparisons, certainly if the journal has a worldwide circulation. Some students prefer to write their articles with their supervisors and/or with other authors who are adept at getting themselves published (see the section in Chapter 3 on 'Whose Work is it Anyway?'). It is also important not to feel upset if your article is rejected, but to read the feedback from independent reviewers properly so that you can improve your output and seek other journals that may be in a position to accept your paper. If you are unsure of what went wrong with your article, you can ask for advice from the editor, who will give you guidance on where else to publish if the rejection is final.

Conference paper

Writing for a conference can be a taxing experience, particularly if you are asked to contribute to published proceedings; your work will usually be scrutinised by specialists who will ask for changes that will fit well with the themes of the proceedings. It is important to attend some of the other papers that are being presented and evaluate what the audience feels like and to glean as much information as you can on the style and focus of the other presentations.

You would have prepared in advance and practised your paper, but you might be better enlightened as to exactly what is expected whilst in the thick of the conference itself. For example, if many of those attending are not speakers of English as their first language, as often happens in international conferences, you might need to clarify certain terms more than you would if you were addressing only native speakers of the language. You will also need to stick to time and allow space for questions at the end of your session. The important aspect to keep in mind is never to assume that your audience will be familiar with the content of what you are saying. Unlike an in-house seminar or workshop with your peers and tutors, in a conference, you might be addressing all kind of audiences, young and old, experienced and not, including students, professors or even sometimes members of the community or other stakeholders, such as interested professionals, who will not necessarily be used to an abstract or academic way of presenting research. The key is to be explicit, accessible and clear, whilst keeping to an adequate pace (neither too slow nor too rushed) that gives everyone the opportunity to absorb the main points you are making.

English for academic purposes (EAP)

English for academic purposes (or EAP) is a language system with its own rules, conventions and guardians, the written and spoken works of your tutors and journal referees being good examples of these. We would like to propose a functional view of what this language system is about. In Figure 6.1, we try to show the hierarchy of functions that can be understood to emanate from a common and deep component of knowledge and argument in order to address a thesis. This thesis and its constituting elements are always supported by research evidence, a key element in EAP. This deep component and its constituents are realised physically through texts and other outputs with the key intentions (or functions) of dialogue (with the literature on the one hand, the audience on the other, and the reflective 'I' in the middle), argument, presentation, critique and theorising. These deeper intentions are translated via what we have called meta-functions (see the section above in this chapter on 'The Linguistic Skills Needed at Postgraduate Level') at text level. The latter are akin to what you will find within the assessment criteria for postgraduate work.

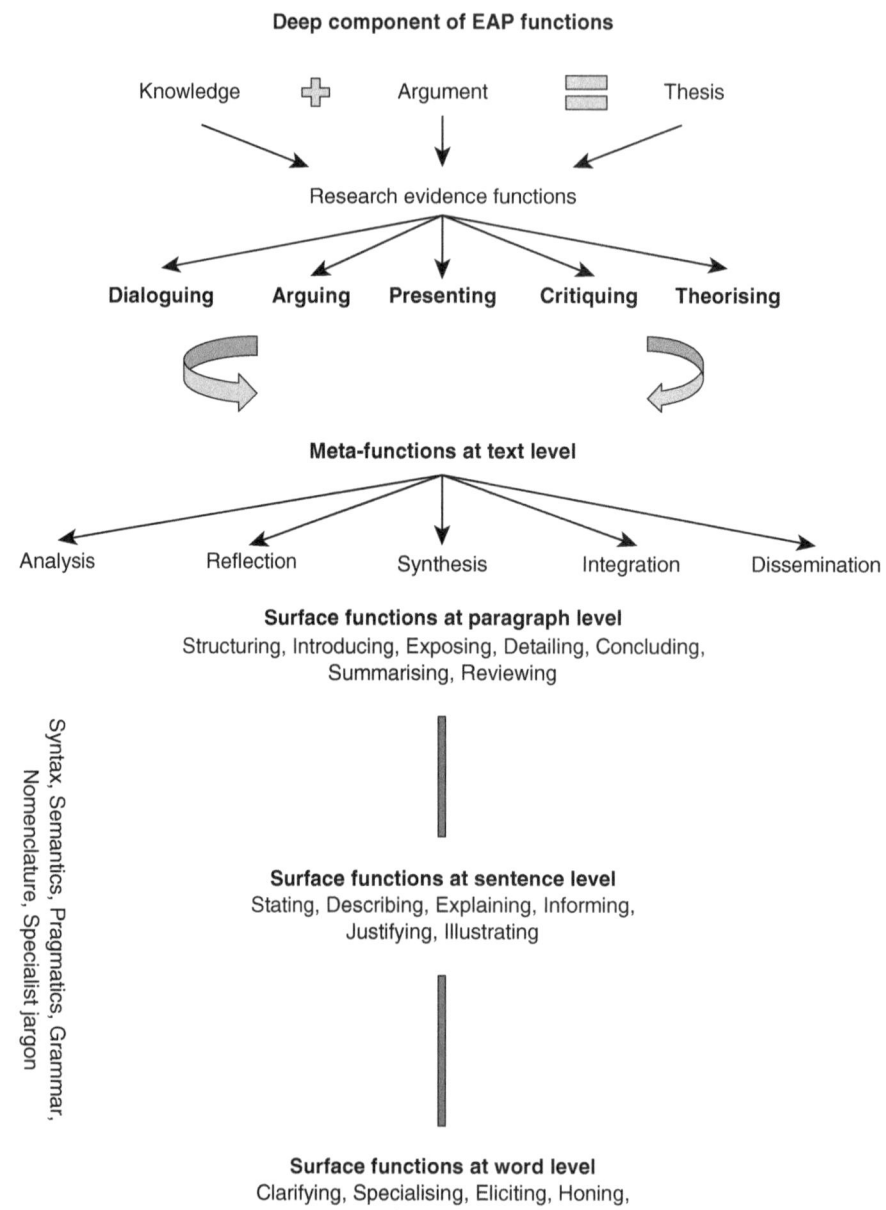

FIGURE 6.1 English for academic purposes (EAP): A hierarchical functional engine

We have added the meta-function of 'dissemination' in order to stress the need for academic work at postgraduate level to be of publishable value. The argument here is always to aim for your work to reach and convince the right readership and audience, whether you are after gaining a qualification or aiming to be published in a book or journal. These meta-functions lead to further realisations, which we have termed 'surface' functions (see Figure 6.1) and tried to address differently (although not necessarily exclusively) for the various levels of writing, from paragraph to sentence to word. Alongside the features pertaining to text are some of the tools needed for constructing well-balanced academic texts such as syntax and semantics.

This model emphasises the importance of drafting, polishing and addressing the complex nature of academic writing with a purpose. Some say that writing academically is far more difficult than any other style of writing. This may or may not be true, however, we can confidently say that academic writing improves with practice, review and re-drafting. The key here is to immerse yourself in the enjoyment of this kind of writing or presenting and develop a discipline for excellence in meeting the criteria and using the language confidently.

Key ideas and terms

Discourse relates to the body of text, spoken or written, to communicate specific knowledge and information. It is codified and has a community pertaining to it. A given discourse has its own rules of content and form. For example, we speak of the discourses of teenagers, of sport, of politicians, of science and of feminism, among many other forms or subforms of a given discourse. Academic discourse in the Social Sciences tends to follow a set of linguistic conventions, utilising the skills or functions of analysis, synthesis and reflection, as well as highly specialised and precise vocabulary.

Pragmatics, semantics and syntax These are rules that govern the way in which we use language at deeper levels and vary according to the discourse, the context, the situation and any other aspect that might impact on language use. For example, the statement 'It's cold in here' (which, at surface level, functions as a description or a statement of perceived reality) could also mean any of the following interpretations and their functions: 'It's cold in here!' (intended as a complaint); or 'Close the window' (an order); or 'Shall we choose another room?' (an invitation); or even perhaps 'This would be an ideal place for operating my computer, which is overheating' (a statement). Academic written language tends to utilise the function of statement (i.e., stating the 'what' of a given intellectual enquiry) more than is evident in everyday language. In that sense, academic language is perceived as rather rigid, formal and very precise. In its spoken form, however, it may use rhetorical devices, which allow for more flexibility with the functions of, for example, invitation, request and complaint.

Hedging relates to a way of using language to convey meaning in a less direct and less categorical manner. It is very prevalent in academic discourse where either grammatical forms are used to temper an argument (e.g., 'I wonder if it would be at all possible …' versus 'Would it be possible …') or words are added to make statements less categorical (e.g., 'It is perhaps useful to consider …' versus 'It is useful to consider …').

A functional system is about how the English language relates to how we communicate intentions via texts (whether long, short, oral or written). The statement 'It's cold in here' is grammatically simple, but functionally potentially more complex than what it seems to denote (as in the example given at the start of this section). The syntactic structure of 'It's cold in here' is a fairly common English one of:

$$pronoun + verb + complement + adverb$$

and is similar to countless other ones (e.g., the statement 'She is funny most of the time' has exactly the same syntactic structure as that of 'It's cold in here'). However, the function of 'It's cold in here' is not necessarily that of a statement of description, but could well be intended as a complaint or an order, depending on the pragmatics and the semantics of the situation and context in which it was produced. In formal academic writing this is mostly avoided, as ambiguity is not conducive to communicating knowledge clearly to an audience. In academic speaking, however, some pragmatics can be a good hook for engaging an audience.

Meta-functions relate to how academic language, especially in the fields of the Humanities and Social Sciences, deeply converges towards a set of understood criteria or skills around analysis, reflection, critique and synthesis. These could be seen as being the overarching intentions of texts and their authors or, indeed, the meta-functions behind all the texts produced within these fields of enquiry.

English for academic purposes (EAP) is a discourse which obeys some formalised rules of using English that are not those necessarily found in everyday English. There are devices used such as 'premodifiers' and 'nominalisations' that are invaluable for succinct and clear language. EAP also has a very specialised or professional vocabulary which pertains to an academic community that specialises in the knowledge-making and development of particular fields of enquiry, or subjects and disciplines.

Nomenclature is the lexis (or set of words and names) associated with a specific field of study and subject. It is highly specialised and describes particular ideas, concepts, constructs and arguments. There are diverse nomenclatures that follow the different subjects that exist in the Social Sciences, as well as professional discourses, such as in Management, Education and Health, which have their own terminologies.

Chapter summary

This chapter explains the structure of language so that you will be able to work on enhancing the basic linguistic skills of writing, reading, speaking and listening. Key to this is understanding that there are significant differences between everyday language (generally informal) and formal academic writing or speaking, which require depth of analysis, critique, reflection and synthesis. This form of language that is necessary for postgraduate study can be learnt. It is the core element of pre-sessional courses widely provided for international students. Good preparation for postgraduate study will involve reading academic articles and books in your field, as well as attending conference papers on your subject or those allied to it. We advise you to buy a specialist dictionary for your subject and to pick it up from time to time to familiarise yourself with the specialist language of your field of study. Outstanding written work requires careful drafting and redrafting, polishing every single paragraph, sentence and word in order to create a coherent whole that reads very well. Critical friends are invaluable in helping you to write with clarity, and this is more to do with simplicity and precision than with over-complicated language and expression. Oral presentations can become a daunting part of postgraduate courses, but we explain how to engage your audience through planning and structuring the content, and through paying attention to voice, eye contact and well-worked-out visual and/or audio material. During your course, as well as presentations, there will be a variety of written tasks that you will be required to handle, so we go through the features and differences between assignments, dissertation, thesis, article and conference paper. The overall features and characteristics of English for academic purposes (EAP) are summarised in a model that relates the different elements to each other.

7

Preparing Your Dissertation or Thesis Proposal

Chapter overview

In this chapter, we will go through the steps that you will need to take in order to prepare a dissertation or thesis proposal. Carrying out each step will enable you to complete a draft proposal that you will be able to discuss with your tutor. We begin with the important question of choosing a topic. Our strong advice is to draw on your personal and, if relevant, professional experience in choosing a topic that is interesting and relevant to you, has a wider or more general importance, lends itself to systematic study, and is achievable with the resources and time available. Choosing to focus on a workplace setting can be helpful because you can bring some familiarity, knowledge and professional understanding to the research context. We emphasise the necessity of obtaining ethical approval before you undertake any research involving human participants, and only when it has been granted can you proceed with sending out letters, carrying out observations or conducting interviews. Once completed, sections of the proposal can be used as the building blocks for Chapter 1 of your thesis or dissertation, which provides an overview of the study. The chapter builds directly on the structure, text and dissertation planning framework developed by Professor Michael Crossley at the University of Bristol, Graduate School of Education (*Planning and Writing a Dissertation: Working with Your Adviser*, undated). We have worked with Michael in using this approach with our own postgraduate students and are pleased to acknowledge how this has inspired the current chapter.

Topic of study

Most universities and colleges require the postgraduate student to set out a proposal for their **dissertation** or **thesis**. A dissertation or thesis is an extended and detailed academic study of a single topic or area within the broad compass of the postgraduate degree. 'Dissertation' is the word usually used to describe this study in the context of a taught degree whilst 'thesis' is usually used for a postgraduate research degree. They are really interchangeable and, for ease of use, we will use the term 'dissertation' to cover both.

Writing a dissertation requires rigour, determination and good time management. A dissertation is an opportunity for you to demonstrate 'mastery'. This means being able to show the reader your skill of integrating past and present knowledge, and your discovery of new knowledge. The model of dissertation should be decided, depending on whether you are undertaking a literature-based dissertation or attempting to discover new knowledge. In both cases, a clear, concise structure is helpful to guide the reader through the dissertation. While there are many different ways to structure a dissertation, what follows is a model structure that can easily be adapted to suit most topics of study. However, other structures are perfectly acceptable, and you should always consider carefully the advice of your tutors when planning your dissertation.

There are three steps to identifying a suitable topic, the first being to **choose the right topic of study**. Why is this important? By identifying a broad area of research, you are able to 'funnel' the literature until you are left with the literature that is most pertinent to the question being asked. This should be related to your interests and professional experience. It should also be in an area or issue in which you have relevant research materials and references available. The starting point then for deciding what your dissertation should be about is likely to fall in one of two areas. Many students who go on a postgraduate course have spent a period of time working in a professional area such as Health or Business or Education. In this case, it is possible that you will have encountered questions or issues about your professional practice or that of colleagues that might be suitable for a postgraduate dissertation. The same goes for those who apply to do a research degree, and, in fact, many students choose to study a subject and topic that is closely allied to their past or current work experience. Choosing to focus upon a workplace setting can give you an advantage because having an understanding of the geography, culture and routines of the setting is useful to help you navigate your way through processes and procedures that can consume a great deal of your time and energy.

Second, you need to decide on the nature of the more specific issue or problem that you intend to address (see also the 'forest to leaf' discussion in Chapter 5). The exact nature of the issue or problem does not have to be detailed exactly at this stage without some discussion with a tutor who will have been assigned to supervise the dissertation. The tutor's role in this is to begin from where a student is, explore with them their ideas and interests and help them to come up with a working title that is manageable and realistic for a dissertation study. A working title that is adaptable and changeable is useful because, as you read and develop ideas, so, too, should the title as this is part of the research journey. So, the third stage in developing the dissertation topic is likely to be an iterative one, which is refined and reached through discussion with your tutor (Student Example 7.1).

Student example 7.1   Drafting a working title

Cathy is a nurse and is following a taught Master's degree through work-based learning in professional practice. The first step is to decide her topic of study, so she settles on Patient Care. Cathy is, in fact, a specialist nurse and wants to develop her career in this direction. She decides that the more specific issue or problem that she wants to explore in her study is the contribution of the specialist nurse to caring for patients. She has observed specialist nurses working in an NHS ward for patients with rheumatoid arthritis and has been impressed by the value that specialist nurses add to the well-being and recovery of their patients. She drafts a working title that reflects the exact focus of the proposed study:

> What is the Value of the Specialist Nurse in a Team and Does Their Role Enhance Patient Care and Have an Impact on Patient Satisfaction? A Small-Scale Case Study of the Rheumatoid Arthritis Nurse

This is a working title that has been agreed between Cathy and her tutor. It was arrived at after some discussion and after having identified that Cathy had a deep interest in becoming a senior specialist nurse and had experience of specialist nurse practice when working in a team in an NHS hospital. Thus, the topic meets several criteria: it reflects Cathy's personal interest; it follows her professional interest and expertise; it seeks to investigate a real-life question that has significance for Cathy, for the nursing profession and hospital management generally; it connects with a significant range of theoretical, specialist and policy literature; it is 'doable', being a small-scale case study; and it is an achievable study since it uses the resources of the workplace where Cathy is based and it seeks to investigate the common work practices of Cathy and her colleagues in the team. This study has the added advantage of having the potential to generate implications for theory, policy and practice.

Rationale for the study

The rationale for the study is important because it is a statement or, more accurately, a number of statements, explaining to the reader why the study is important. The rationale is also an opportunity to make the point about the complexity of the research and also the apparent gaps in research that have aroused your curiosity and motivated you to investigate the area. It is also an opportunity to briefly inform the reader about how your research will fill a void and how it will impact on the area that you wish to research. So, the rationale explains why you have chosen the topic and focus for the dissertation, saying:

1. Why is the topic of general importance?
    It may be helpful to continue with the example of the specialist nursing in Student Example 7.1, above. However, for topics that are perhaps not as closely aligned with a professional field or occupation, it will be useful to remember that importance in terms of an area of study can be as much about filling gaps in the existing knowledge or connecting two different fields of study, as about more vocationally specific themes. Equally, topics of study that are professionally or occupationally oriented may also be described in terms of their academic contribution, in addition to their utility in the world of work.

> Making a contribution to healthcare that is patient focused, effective and efficient.
>
> At this level, the rationale simply gives the area of experience that the study pertains to, i.e., healthcare, and an indication of its direction, in this case, patient care and sustainability.

2. Why is it of current importance in the context/country that you intend to study?

> Cathy identified a number of areas of current importance to which her her study could contribute. She summarised these as follows:
>
> > The UK government has called for better medical diagnosis, treatment and after-care as people live longer, creating increased demands on healthcare budgets. Research evidence suggests that specialist nurses working in hospitals can significantly improve patient outcomes. There is little existing academic work on the particular contribution of rheumatoid arthritis nurse specialists to patient care teams.
>
> Notice that Cathy's statement on the current importance of the topic refers to government policy and the pressure of the healthcare budget on national finances, broad research evidence on the general topic, and a gap in the research literature covering the specific healthcare area that is the focus of the dissertation proposal. By alluding to both policy and theoretical (i.e., research literature) concerns, this rationale is given additional weight.

3. Why is it important for you?
    Here, we seek to link the topic to our personal interests, skills, professional experience, future career or other individual factors that might serve to strengthen the personal rationale for undertaking this particular study.

> I trained as an adult nurse and, in my first job, decided that I wanted to specialise in the care and rehabilitation of arthritis patients. I have subsequently become a specialist nurse in a large NHS hospital and have decided to explore in my dissertation the value of the specialist nurse within a team and whether their role enhances patient care and has an impact on patient satisfaction. This will increase my confidence as a specialist nurse, enable me to better describe and explain my role to patients, and to demonstrate the added value that my specialism will bring to hospitals and patients. The dissertation will also help me to understand some of the theoretical ideas that underpin my specialism and be exposed to a wider variety of approaches and techniques.

As well as explaining to the reader why the study is important, some careful thought about your rationale for choosing a topic of study should help you ensure that your interest and enthusiasm will be maintained throughout the study. It is not uncommon that students will come to loathe their topic by the end of their studies, familiarity breeding contempt. Being able to remind yourself about why the topic is important to you personally and about its wider importance may just help to keep such negative thoughts at bay.

Research aims and objectives

Identify the **aim** (or aims) of your research. These are working aims and may change as your work progresses. Keep this concise and tightly focused because your dissertation must be realistic in scope and you will have limited resources and time at your disposal. Then list five or six research **objectives**. These are more specific in nature. Remember that one objective common to all dissertations is a critical review of the relevant literature. A second objective is often to produce an overview of the context of your study. The third one could then be to carry out a detailed case study of X, Y or Z. Other objectives could relate to implications for policy and practice, and implications for the existing theoretical literature (to challenge or support it) and for future research.

Aim

To investigate through a small-scale case study the value of the specialist rheumatoid arthritis nurse within a team and whether their role enhances patient care and has an impact on patient satisfaction

Objectives

In the field of specialist nursing and patient care, to:

1. Complete a review of the literature.
2. Review current policy and practice.
3. Carry out a small-scale case study of the rheumatoid arthritis nurse within an NHS hospital team, using structured observation, focus group interviews and content analysis.
4. Make recommendations for specialist nurse care practice in hospital settings.
5. Identify any potential for changes in policy in order to improve patient care.
6. Contribute to, and, if appropriate, challenge the theoretical literature.

The exact wording of your aim and objectives is likely to shift slightly as your study progresses. Research is about progress and change, and writing a dissertation is an iterative process as you learn and become more knowledgeable and confident in your field. It is a very good idea to revisit your aim and objectives periodically because it is quite easy to become sidetracked on some aspect of the study that at the time appears interesting or diverting. On the one hand, you need to acquire the discipline to keep to the study plan, expressed in the aim and objectives. However, on the other hand, recognise that the study is organic and grows and develops along with you, the writer. So, there is a balance to be kept here – flexibility and discipline are both needed, one drawing on creativity skills, the other on organisational skills.

Research questions

In the light of the above, it may then be appropriate to formulate a number of key research questions. Again, keep these concise, tightly focused and realistic.

The general aims, research objectives and specific research questions that you formulate will help you to narrow a broad field into a realistic project for your dissertation. This will also help you to demarcate exactly what literature is appropriate for you to review and use to shape your own critique and analysis.

Research questions

1. What does the theoretical literature say about the role of the specialist nurse in hospital teams?
2. Is there any specific literature on the role of the rheumatoid arthritis nurse?
3. What are the benefits of the specialist nurse working as part of a wider team rather than seeing referrals individually?
4. What improvements in care practice can be identified through a small-scale case study of integrated team-working?
5. Are there any wider implications of such a study for policy, theory and practice?

Theoretical framework

In this section, you outline briefly what theoretical literature you will use in order to guide the research and act as a starting point. A full review of the literature usually follows in the second chapter of your dissertation.

The place to begin is with your paradigm, or underlying theoretical framework. This is important because it describes what will count as knowledge and understanding in your study, and this is what will distinguish your writing as a piece of scholarship rather than as anecdote or journalism. So, the paradigm will comprise your frame of reference for the study, and you will be required to say what this is and, in doing so, to refer to the theoretical literature. This will form the spine of your literature review, to which you will add the specialist literature in your field, including any relevant policy literature. At this point, you may wish to reread the section in Chapter 4 on 'Dealing with Theoretical Literature'.

Your aims, objectives and research questions will have arisen in the light of your reading of the literature of some kind, in combination with your own ideas and professional experience. You must say what this literature is and identify and define the main points of view, concepts and terminology that you will use. While the perspective that you adopt for your study and the concepts that you apply may be derived from the work of other writers, it will become the basis of your own **theoretical framework**.

Historically, two paradigms, 'positivism' and 'constructivism', have had a most significant influence on the way in which research in Education, Management and Professional Studies is carried out. The 'positivist' paradigm is identified with traditional scientific research, which typically relies on empirical study supported by statistical analysis in order to make generalisations based on the research findings. The positivist paradigm is strongly associated with quantitative research methodology that uses methods such as surveys and questionnaires that report through statistical analysis. Positivist researchers maintain that in order to have knowledge about the social world, it is necessary to gather observable and measurable facts, largely using methods drawn from the natural and physical sciences. People are regarded as the objects of research, the researcher is independent of the research subjects, and values should remain external to the research. Research of this kind typically relies on quantitative numerical data that are subjected to inferential statistical analysis to make predictions about future patterns and events.

The 'constructivist' paradigm is identified with qualitative research methodology that largely uses methods drawn from the Social Sciences such as observation and in-depth interviewing, which report through description. To this view, people construct their own knowledge and understanding of the world through their experience and their reflection on that experience. Knowledge is not fixed or static, the preserve of experts, but is living and dynamic and created by participants in social settings. Hence, this orientation is often also termed 'interpretivist', since it relies on the interpretations of participants in social settings to create understanding about meaning. Interpretivist researchers maintain that to have knowledge about the social world, it is necessary to gather data about language, ideas, feelings and meanings that are then frequently subjected to qualitative analysis so as to generate understandings about human behaviours and interaction. People are regarded as participants in the research, the researcher adopts a reflexive stance to acknowledge involvement in and impact on the research process itself, and values are integral to the research.

A third paradigm that has become influential across the Social Sciences is 'transformational' or 'critical' theory. 'Critical theory' tends to lean towards the more descriptive axis of the interpretive paradigm (although it often combines qualitative and quantitative methodologies). Critical theory arose from a critique of the two paradigms of positivism and constructivism outlined above. It has critiqued them for the insufficient acknowledgement and inclusion of issues of power, race and gender and aims to achieve a closer connection between research and politics, especially the agenda of diversity of values and social positions.

Student example 7.2   Choosing the paradigm

In principle, in the generic field of specialist nursing and patient care, either positivist or constructivist paradigms could be employed. Reflective practice in Health research, as well as in other Social Sciences, is an influential method within the constructivist paradigm. This will allow the researcher: to place her study within a well-known and

(Continued)

recognisable theoretical research tradition; to draw on comparable research findings from studies elsewhere; to link her study to past and current health policy; and to employ a method that is appropriate and suitable for the postgraduate dissertation. Given that Cathy's study is to be completed for the purposes of a postgraduate course, with limited time and resources available, and that the focus of interest is a small nursing team, the small-scale case study approach would seem to be the most appropriate. More specifically, this study can perhaps best be achieved by Cathy examining her own practice and also that of other specialist nurses working on her ward. For the postgraduate student, a key consideration is that of time and practicality: which areas of work will she have access to and which can be best monitored within a short timescale, with maximum effect in terms of gathering evidence. In our example, the benefits of including the researcher's own practice in the study are apparent. Many professional studies carried out as part of a higher degree programme will share these features, which accounts for the popularity of the small-scale case study as a principal method in Social Science dissertations.

Having decided on the overarching paradigm and the body of theoretical literature to support this, you will need to consider which specialist research literature to include (Student Example 7.3).

Student example 7.3   Choosing the specialist research literature

In Cathy's study, the specialist research literature has been partly identified in the objectives: to review current policy and practice in the field of specialist nursing and patient care. In the research questions, we added to this: specific literature on the role of the rheumatoid arthritis nurse. This would be a sufficiently broad specialist focus for a postgraduate dissertation study. However, in addition, it will be beneficial to review the policy literature, sometimes referred to as 'grey' literature, for example relevant Department of Health guidelines on specialist nurse care, and anything emanating from the College of Nursing or other professional healthcare bodies. Remember, the university specialist subject librarian will be able to advise you on potential sources of research literature, and may well be able to come up with some ideas that you have not thought of. He or she may need a little time to carry out some investigative research on your behalf. Therefore, it is a good idea to build this timeframe into your research schedule.

In summary, the literature review will begin with a discussion of your paradigm (the spine). Remember to say why you have chosen it and why it is the most suitable option. Then, there is the literature of your specialist field. This might be the history of careers education in secondary schools for the educationalist, or for the management student it might be a comparison of approaches to marketing. Then, there is the policy literature that helps to contextualise the study in its social, political and professional setting. We gave more guidance on choosing relevant literature in Chapter 4.

Remember that in the conclusion to your study, your findings should be related back to the literature in order to support or challenge existing knowledge.

Research methodology and methods

What is the **research methodology** that you will use in your research? Remember that 'research methodology' is not the same as **research method**, although you will find different writers and university tutors using these and other terms in this section quite interchangeably. Try not to let this confuse you. The key point to understand is that you need to begin with the wider philosophical wrap-around, whatever that is termed. Methodology is derived from the paradigm or theoretical framework that describes how you view the world as a person and as a researcher (see the previous section).

'Methodology' is the overall approach to research: quantitative or qualitative or transformational.

'Method' is the research approach that you will use to collect and analyse your data. Examples of methods are: survey, case study and ethnography. Sometimes, mixed methods are employed. These can, for example, sit wholly within a qualitative methodology, or can draw on both qualitative and quantitative methodologies. Within each research method, you will have a choice of a number of **research techniques and instruments**. Examples of these, used in many student dissertations, are structured and semi-structured interview, questionnaire and content analysis.

Now, we can see that there is a strong hierarchical relationship between paradigm, or theoretical framework, research methodology, generally quantitative or qualitative, research method, and data collection tools and techniques. Essentially, it is the paradigm or theoretical framework that determines the methodology that provides the rationale for one particular method over another. A common mistake is for students to home in on a research technique without giving serious thought to the overarching paradigm and the methodology that flows from that. It is all too common to hear, 'I want to do an interview study of Health Centre users' or 'I want to do a Q-sort of English teachers' or 'I want to give a questionnaire to Year 9.' The point is that these decisions should come at the end of the process of designing the study, not at the beginning. Student Example 7.4 may help to make this clear.

Student example 7.4   Rationale for the choice of paradigm

Mayumi is planning a study of six women managers in a government office with the aim of understanding their lived experiences of the glass ceiling and career advancement. The study draws principally on the constructivist paradigm and utilises qualitative methodology, primarily the methods of the in-depth semi-structured interview and the focus group. The rationale for the choice of paradigm is that the study seeks to access the women's own understandings and interpretations of their work and social setting. This then requires a qualitative methodology because the research aims to give an account of the women's own work experiences and then relate this to their career development and aspirations. It is principally through the rich description provided by the in-depth interview method that their perspectives can be accessed. The method is contained, convenient and doable. The focus group method offers a further dimension because it is held to be likely that the women responding as a group will generate elements of consensus, divergence and priority in relation to the issues at hand. It is more than possible that a transformative paradigm (see the previous section) will emerge for this study if the research is driven by the firm view that the women's opportunities have been limited by wider social and political factors such as gender stereotypes, unequal salary structures or restricted access to professional development opportunities, and Mayumi hopes that the study will contribute to change.

This section has conflated a discussion of methodology and method with the theoretical literature. This is deliberate because we believe that it is the grounding of the study in the relevant theoretical literature that distinguishes academic writing from other kinds of writing, and the extent to which you successfully do this will have a big impact on the quality of your work. Research methodology is often spoken and written about rather loosely, within academia as well as outside it, so we have tried to clarify and describe an approach to methodology and associated theoretical literature that will provide a sound basis for a well-written and scholarly dissertation.

Research ethics

Research ethics is the most important aspect of any research project that involves collecting empirical data. Before you undertake any research involving human participants, ethical approval must be sought, and only when it has been granted can you proceed with sending out your letters, carrying out observations or conducting interviews. Carrying out research with human participants is a privilege. You will be asking respondents to share aspects of their lives with you, sometimes information that is personal, sensitive and confidential; you will have, as a researcher, **a duty of care** towards them. There are strong and inviolable ethical imperatives that flow from this which include, but transcend, the normal discourse of confidentiality that surrounds research ethics discussions. Not every ethical circumstance can be anticipated. However, adequate measures must be in place to deal with any circumstances that can compromise the research, the researcher or the participants. Often, your institution will provide an ethics checklist in which you can discuss how you have dealt with, or plan to deal with any ethical issues related to your study. You could also use this to frame your initial tutorial with your appointed supervisor. If you require access to an institution, such as a school or workplace, written permission will be needed. If ethical guidelines exist in your subject area, these should always be followed; for example, in education, researchers follow those prepared by the British Educational Research Association (BERA, see www.bera.ac.uk/wp-content/uploads/2014/02/BERA-Ethical-Guidelines-2011.pdf). If you are carrying out research in the NHS, special ethical procedures must be followed.

If you are carrying out research in your own organisation, perhaps interviewing or observing colleagues, remember to ensure that you deal with the ethical dimensions of your changed role. By this, we mean that in carrying out research in your workplace, you are placing yourself in a different relationship from those you normally have when interacting as a colleague or manager. One of the key ethical principles is that of **informed consent**, that is: that your participants are aware of what you are doing; aware of how they are expected to participate; are completely comfortable with their involvement; and feel that they can withdraw from the process at any time without any detriment to themselves. This requires very careful handling, especially if you are observing or questioning those who may report to you. As their supervisor or manager, there is a particular power relationship between you. As you become a researcher, this relationship changes, and your duty of care requires that you thoughtfully consider what you will need to say and do in order to avoid taking advantage of those you manage. At the very least, you will need to ensure that participants are clear about what exactly is expected of them. Researching in your own organisation can uncover, and sometimes deliberately so, issues that are sensitive, for example relating to the actions and behaviours of others in the organisation. Your duty of care will include ensuring that anonymity is preserved, not only for individuals, but also for the organisation itself. Your proposal should make clear how you will deal with the issue of confidentiality, and also the wider issues noted above that flow from a duty of care, including the well-being of all participants in the study, and of yourself as the researcher.

A final but important consideration is the question of researcher bias. This is the matter of ensuring that the researcher's own views and preferences are, as far as possible, not imposed on participants and unthinkingly confirmed by the research. It is also vital to acknowledge where the research may be influenced, perhaps by the pre-existing relationship between the researcher and the participants in the study, or by the researcher's pre-existing professional knowledge and experience. The best research takes special care not to impose the assumptive world of the researcher upon the study and its participants.

NB You can turn the above sections into the first chapter of your dissertation (called 'Introduction') if you add an extra section titled 'Overview of the Study'.

Sources of data

In this section, you should identify your main sources of data, materials and references.

At an early stage of your planning, you must at least know where the information that you will need will be coming from. It is a good idea to list main sources. This might remind you to write to various official bodies/people for important material. This must be done at the outset, if replies are to be in time to influence the shape and nature of the study.

Some research approaches that handle large amounts of data such as certain questionnaire studies may need to make use of a database. Choosing one that is most suited to the purpose and needs of the study requires some early planning, thought and care. Databases can save time and be a real help in the organisation and analysis of data, but only if they are fit for purpose. If not, they can be, at best, a distraction and, at worst, jeopardise the smooth progress of the study.

If your study involves work-based research, in your own organisation or externally, you will need to allow time to obtain the necessary permissions to collect data. If you plan to use a questionnaire, you should build in an opportunity to pilot the questionnaire instrument with a small group whose characteristics are not unlike your proposed sample. You will need to give thought to who this group will be and how you will contact them, and then how you will administer the questionnaire itself. Most postgraduate research is time constrained, that is, there is a fixed deadline before which you have to submit your dissertation. Bearing this in mind, always allow plenty of contingency time for late responses or possibly having to change plans or direction. The old maxim, 'failing to plan is planning to fail', applies here.

Production schedule

Map out a timetable for your work. Include all the months that you will have available. Against each month, write in the dissertation tasks that you plan to do in that time. Remember, writing up the dissertation takes more than one draft. Many universities expect students to prepare a Gantt chart, illustrating this process visually. This is a useful tool in helping you to keep on schedule, and helps as a reminder of which tasks you need to do and when. Be sure to build in contingency time to allow for unforeseen circumstances, unplanned events, unexpected delays and overruns, for example through illness or other pressures on your time.

DRAWING 7.1   Running against four clocks

Often, your university department or graduate school will have a preferred way for students to present their planned work timetable; of course, in this case, you should follow the preferred method. Above all, do not worry if you have to change your plans. Frequently, academic study can take off in an unexpected direction. Often, these are not major changes that would require you to submit a new dissertation proposal, but rather additional elements or changes of focus here and there. All plans should be flexible, so the main thing is to carefully think through the implications of any changes, and to make sure that you can still meet your aims and objectives. Seek advice from your tutor if you are worried that you may not be on track, as they are there to help.

Draft table of contents

Drafting a table of contents with chapter titles, headings and possible sub-headings can be useful in helping you plan and get organised. This will change throughout the study, but it is very helpful to have a working draft early on. We recommend that you spend some time whilst working up your own pro-posal, taking a look at successfully completed Master's dissertations and Doctoral theses. These can be found in your university library or online and, by looking at those in your subject area, you will gain a useful overview of the scope and possible structure for your own proposal. There is user-friendly software available that can help you prepare a detailed list of contents with headings for sub-sections and so on. We recommend that you number your headings as it makes for easier cross-referencing and querying. Do not write the numbers manually as you type your headings, but use Microsoft Word's automatic function for numbering headings. This will also enable figure and table captions to generate numbers based on the chapters.

Working list of references

The first draft for your emerging list of references that you submit with your proposal should indicate only the main references that you are currently aware of. This could be one to two pages in length at this preliminary stage.

A major consideration is the areas of your proposal that you will need to support with scholarly references. In general, there are three key areas where you should seek to use authoritative sources to support your work. The first is the general context of the study. In all areas of Education, Management and Professional Studies this will involve seeking out influential reports or seminal works that signal important professional developments and changes in policy direction. Government reports will often feature here, as will major reviews of professional standards or training (grey literature). These sources will set the tone of your study and contextualise it within its social, economic and political setting. A simple Google search will help you to find relevant sources, although Google will not help you to identify what is most signifi-cant, relevant or important. For that, you must use your own professional knowledge and judgement. A useful practical way to get started with the policy literature is to identify a key source, say a seminal government or academic report produced for a government department or professional body. In this, you will be able to track down further key references that the authors have relied on to draft their work. In this way, you can gradually come to understand which sources really are central, and thus know about the ones you will do well to include in your dissertation.

The second area is your paradigm. There are several different terms that have shades of meaning that are similar to and different from a 'paradigm', including 'theoretical orientation' and 'hermeneutic', but they are all used more or less interchangeably in the research literature. We will use the term 'paradigm'. This is really about the major philosophical influences on your approach that influence the way in which knowledge is studied and interpreted. It is important to give careful thought to the major theoretical influences on your proposal when constructing the list of references, and to use the original texts where possible. For example, it is better to cite an influential scholar, such as Pierre Bourdieu, in their field rather than an author who has cited Bourdieu in their work. Even if you first came across Bourdieu's work in a later scholar's writing, if you can and if you have time, seek out the original thinker's work in the library and use that for your citations, if possible. Examiners like to see that a candidate has taken care to chase down the original sources rather than the secondary ones.

The third major aspect of your dissertation proposal for which you will need authoritative sources is for the specialist topics that are included in your research questions. This is the area where, if you are studying at doctoral level, you will be aiming to make a substantive contribution to the theoretical literature. So, your references will need to include those authors who have contributed the major thinking on and around your topic, and it is in describing, questioning and, in some cases, challenging these sources that you will define your own distinct contribution to the knowledge in your field.

Using one of the software packages such as Endnote, which can be used to cite and format references in a manuscript, and works well with Microsoft Word, may take a little time to learn and get used to, but can save time in the long run and help to ensure that your references are organised, complete and properly formatted.

Key ideas and terms

Dissertation and **thesis** are terms often used interchangeably to describe an extended piece of work that develops a critical argument within the student's subject field. 'Dissertation' is the word usually used to describe this study in the context of a taught degree, whilst 'thesis' is usually used for a postgraduate research degree. In this book, we mainly use the term 'dissertation'.

Choosing the right topic of study is crucial to a successful dissertation. The topic should ideally link closely to your interests and professional experience, should define a specific issue or problem that is suitable for a research investigation, and should be refined through discussion with your tutor/supervisor.

The aim of a research study should be concise and tightly focused on the key purpose of the study. The aim may change as your work progresses but it should always encapsulate what aspect of life will be changed or improved as a consequence of the study.

Objectives are more specific and state how the aim will be achieved through different aspects of the study, such as carrying out a case study and building on and challenging the existing theoretical literature.

The theoretical framework describes the paradigm of the study, for example positivist or constructivist. This informs the reader about the overall philosophical approach that you are taking and will largely determine what methodology and method you will employ in carrying out the study.

The research methodology is derived from the theoretical framework and describes the overall approach to your research – quantitative or qualitative or transformational.

The research method is the broad research approach that you will use to collect your data, which might include a survey, a case study and ethnography.

Research techniques and instruments are the technical means by which the data are gathered and may include structured and semi-structured interviews, questionnaires and surveys.

A duty of care exists between researchers and their participants. Sharing personal, sensitive or confidential date with participants is a privilege that carries serious responsibilities. Your study will be shaped and in some ways may be limited by the exact nature of the investigations that you will carry out.

Informed consent requires that your participants are aware of what you are doing, how they are expected to participate, are completely comfortable with their involvement, and feel that they can withdraw from the process at any time without any detriment to themselves.

Chapter summary

This chapter provides a model structure for a dissertation or thesis proposal. It can be used as a template for most taught Master's course dissertations, as well as for professional doctorates and PhDs. The sections are arranged in the order in which you would normally present the different sections of your proposal, and you can use the 11 headings for the sections in this chapter, from 'Topic of Study' through to 'Working List of References' above, in order to write your proposal. The proposal does not have to be long. However, it should incorporate the details in each section, informing the reader of each step that you intend to take, and should give a clear explanation of the methodology and research methods that you plan to use, and also any other relevant information that is necessary to fully brief the supervisor. The good news is that many of the sections of the proposal can be expanded later on to become chapters (e.g., the sections above, from 'Topic of Study' to 'Research Ethics', can be converted into a first draft of the first chapter for most dissertations).

8

Next Steps

Chapter overview

This chapter looks at the 'what next?' aspect of your postgraduate studies. Once you have tackled the initial hurdles and are well underway with your course, you will need to start to consider where those studies might lead you. If you are planning a future in academia, it is good to start thinking about how you might establish yourself in the field. This might include the development of your social profile and your first publications. It may be that you have completed a Master's and are now interested in pursuing a doctorate or that you just want to know how your Master's will help in your employment. A number of aspects are explored in this chapter. But first it is important to realise that even after you have tackled the initial 'imposter syndrome', there will still be additional trials at postgraduate level that you may not have faced before. So, before moving on to the next steps, it may be helpful to acknowledge the potential complexities of postgraduate study and some of the support that is in place to help you deal with those.

What if things go wrong?

It is far more likely for you to experience setbacks during your time as a postgraduate than it was as an undergraduate. This is because you will probably be managing your academic work alongside a myriad of other responsibilities. At postgraduate level, you are far more likely to be juggling paid employment and family responsibilities, and this can cause countless problems and setbacks. But please rest assured that this is part and parcel of the postgraduate culture and those who work within it are empathetic to the many pressures that you are under. It is highly probable that your postgraduate tutors have encountered any number of the complications in the list below when supporting their students:

- Relationship problems
- Caring for ill relatives
- Childcare issues
- Overwhelming work demands
- Pregnancy
- Financial issues
- Personal health (including mental health) issues
- Bereavement
- Crisis of confidence

And these are just a few examples. It is also not uncommon for students to be dealing with a number of issues rather than just one. The important thing to realise is that your tutors are perfectly used to dealing with such matters and will provide a sympathetic ear. These may not be academic issues, but they will impact on your engagement with your studies. Do not be afraid to talk through such issues with your tutors so that they are aware of them and so that they can support you. This may mean them pointing you in the direction of support systems and experts at the university, but it is still good for them to be aware of your circumstances so that they can temper the demands that they place on you. So, if you are struggling with such issues, how can the university help? Below, we discuss some of the support structures that you can access.

Intercalation

Intercalation is a complicated word that simply means to take a break from your studies. It may be called something different in your own institution. Most modular postgraduate study will provide the option for you to take modules as and when it suits you. If you know that there is an extremely busy time in your life approaching, be that to do with your paid employment, marriage, pregnancy, whatever the reason, then give yourself that coming term or semester off. Your registration period should allow you the flexibility to do that.

If you are in the middle of a dissertation or a thesis when you become overwhelmed and unable to cope, then you have the option to intercalate. This means to literally put your studies 'on hold' for a period of time. It may be that you will be required to set a time period, for example, three months, or it may be that you will be permitted to intercalate indefinitely, this will differ from institution to institution. But do not be afraid of having that conversation with your tutor. You may just need a bit of breathing space.

Financial help

It may be that you will find the financial side of things tricky at some point during your studies. The intercalation option above may help you to sort this out, but you may also find that there are alternative methods of paying your fees, for example, monthly rather than termly, that may ease the problem for you. The people to talk to about this are in your institute's Finance Department, as they will be aware of the options open to you. They will also be able to direct you to any funding that might be available to you through, for example, hardship grants or loans. Another avenue to consider if you are studying full-time is to convert to part-time and seek paid employment whilst you are studying in order to help with the bills. This may negate other fees or loans that you have in place, so it would need to be talked through with your institute's financial experts.

Academic support

It may be that you suffer a crisis of confidence in your own ability, or that there is a certain area of study that you find relentlessly difficult. If you are having a crisis of confidence, as we have mentioned in earlier chapters, this is a completely normal aspect of postgraduate study. It can be overwhelming to think that you should be functioning at a certain level of 'academia' when you really do not feel very 'academic' at all. The important thing is to talk it through with your tutors or supervisors and not hide yourself away in the hope that it will disappear – because a lack of contact is only likely to make it worse. The longer you panic, the longer you get nothing achieved and the more behind you feel ... and so, the more you panic. As soon as you begin to feel overwhelmed, let your tutors know; and you can work on small but achievable steps to get you through the difficult time.

If it is something more specific, like an ongoing battle with dyslexia or referencing, then seek help from those who are there to support you, for example writing-support tutors or the librarians. These services are there to support all levels of study. The more complex your study becomes, the more specific your needs become, and these support services are well aware of this.

Emotional support

Anyone who has experienced postgraduate study and, in particular, an extended research project of any kind, is well aware of the emotional labour that this involves. In particular, this is a very isolating time, and, in terms of research, in particular, you are going through an experience that no one else can share. No one else can empathise with your particular situation, no one else can offer advice, as your situation is unique. You are 'on your own' in the truest sense and that can be very destabilising. Your greatest support through this will be your fellow research students who are sharing a similar, if different experience. Another source of support will be your tutors, who will also have encountered very similar experiences. Talk about how you are feeling.

It is really important, if you are finding the emotional side of your study difficult, to realise that this is perfectly normal. Although not discussed nearly as frequently as it should be in research literature, the emotional impact is very real. If you begin to feel overwhelmed, it is important that you do those things that have already been discussed in previous chapters (Chapter 3, for example). Take a break from your studies, switch off, do something completely different with your friends. If that becomes difficult for you and anxiety about your studies becomes all-consuming, then you need to seek help with this. Universities have excellent counsellors who are available through your student services. Make use of them to talk through your particular situation and help you to develop coping strategies (Student Example 8.1).

Student example 8.1   Seeking help and intercalating

Samandeep, who was a postgraduate student and a parent, found herself getting more and more anxious about her lack of progress with her research. The more anxious she became, the more she found herself unable to focus and unable to articulate herself. Samandeep felt that she had now completely lost her grip on where she should be with her research project and was embarrassed about her ineptitude. She became increasingly tired and depressed and found herself making excuses based around her family and exaggerating illness in order to avoid meeting her tutors, her research participants and her fellow students.

Samandeep's tutor contacted her a number of times. Samandeep ignored the first few emails and telephone calls, but the final one was related to a review that was required by the university's Research Degrees Board. Without completing this, her studies would be suspended. Samandeep attended the tutorial and, as soon as her

(Continued)

tutor asked her how she was, she became extremely upset. Her tutor listened whilst she explained how over the last two months she had become increasingly anxious about her work and felt that she could no longer cope with it. She felt that her only option was to give up. Her tutor said that he had wished that she had come to talk to him earlier.

It was agreed that Samandeep needed a break from her studies in order to regain her emotional health. She would intercalate for three months. During that time, she would visit her own GP. She had previously needed medication to cope with anxiety and she would discuss this further with her doctor. Her tutor also gave her the contact details of the counselling service at the university. These counsellors would help her to cope with the anxiety that she was feeling, and work with her on designing ways to better manage her time and responsibilities. She would not be expected to produce any work over those three months, but she could carry on with her own reading if she felt up to it. It was fine if she did not.

It was agreed that her tutor would not contact Samandeep during this time, but that he would be happy to hear from her if she wished to be in touch. With the pressure lifted, Samandeep was able to concentrate on her own health for a while without dealing with the anxiety of her many uncompleted research tasks. When she was well enough to return to her studies, she did so with very clear boundaries and strategies in place for juggling the responsibilities of her different roles as student and parent.

Health issues

If any mental or physical health issues that you have prevent you from studying, then it is important that you apply for **mitigating circumstances** at the first opportunity. 'Mit circs', as they are often abbreviated to, acknowledge your difficulties and provide you time to be able to deal with just those problems and leave the pressure of study behind for a period of time. They are most frequently used to extend submission dates and allow more time to be given for assessments to be completed. But they can also be used to give 'allowance' for a piece of work in terms of performance being affected by illness, physical or mental. The rules and regulations will vary from university to university, but it is probable that some sort of medical evidence will be needed to uphold your claim. This might be a note from your GP or a record of hospital visits. Discuss this option further with your tutor if you feel that your performance has been seriously affected by circumstances, such as ill health, which are beyond your control.

Complaints

Most students look back on their time at university with pleasure and nostalgia. However, sometimes, and rarely, things can go badly wrong and action needs to be taken. If you arrive in a situation where you feel unsafe, uncertain, uncomfortable or in any way unhappy with what you are experiencing at university, always seek advice from the Students' Union or student services. It does not matter whether the issue is with a student, tutor or another person you interact with whilst at university, or to do with the teaching, facilities or services provided by the university. If the matter cannot be resolved informally, then it may be necessary to make a formal complaint, particularly if you feel that you have experienced unfairness or any disadvantage as a result of another person's actions. All universities have detailed **complaints procedures**, and you should feel confident that you will receive a fair hearing and unbiased consideration of your complaint. You have the right to be accompanied by a friend, or a Students' Union officer, in any meeting or hearing. These procedures have several stages, each escalating to a higher level. Ultimately, if your complaint is not satisfactorily resolved by the university, you have the right to ask the ombudsman – in England and Wales, the Office of the Independent Adjudicator for Higher Education (OIA) – to consider your case. The ombudsman can instruct the university to make redress if it finds in your favour. In practice, most complaints are resolved informally.

Having explored some ways in which things could possibly go wrong during your time as a postgraduate, it is time to focus on the positives. You have successfully negotiated all of the hurdles and are well on your way to obtaining your Master's or your PhD. So, what next?

Employability

It may be that you are taking a postgraduate degree that is directly related to your job role or even to you gaining a promotion. In that case, your next steps are already marked out for you. PGCE is one example of a postgraduate certificate that is directly related to becoming employed as a teacher. Frequently, further qualifications in an area such as Business Management are directly related to promotion or progression at work. It is equally likely, though, that you have progressed onto postgraduate-level study simply because you have a passion for the subject, or a love of learning. In this case, it is important that you do not underestimate the wealth of skills that are developed through postgraduate study (see the section below on 'Researcher Development Framework (RDF)'), and that you celebrate these in your CV.

These abilities include (but also go beyond): independent study; time management; presentation skills; communication and collaboration; critical analysis and reflection; subject expertise; research skills; and confidence and resilience. Each of these will now be considered.

Independent study

As we have spent a great deal of time discussing, study at postgraduate level involves a completely different skills-set from study at undergraduate level. You will be making your own decisions about what, exactly, you want to study, and how you will go about it. This involves skills of organisation, critical analysis and decision-making – but, perhaps more importantly, it also involves the initiative to make smart decisions and the commitment and resilience to see these through.

Time management

Postgraduate degrees involve substantial amounts of time doing solitary research. No one is able to direct you in terms of where or when this should happen: you have to create your own timetable. You may have the luxury of full days that can be spent on research or you may be snatching hours around work or family commitments. Either way, identifying suitable times, prioritising and being able to carry out independent study with commitment and consistency, in the absence of external motivators or regulators, is a laudable quality (Student Example 8.2).

Student example 8.2   Devising your own timetable

Simon had come from teaching in a primary school to full-time postgraduate research. Within teaching, every minute of his day was rigidly accounted for with lessons, assemblies, meetings and playground duties. At university, all of his time was his own, apart from the occasional taught session or tutorial. He felt overwhelmed by the lack of externally imposed order and found that he was wasting hours of his time achieving very little. He discovered that in order to use that time most effectively, he needed to devise his own timetable, with short periods of focused time on different aspects of his study. He also made sure that he gave himself regular breaks. Although many of his peers took a far more relaxed approach, these boundaries enabled Simon to use his time far more productively.

Presentation skills

Postgraduate study will usually involve far more than writing essays or dissertations. It will also involve you verbally presenting your work to various audiences. This may be to your peers, tutors or an examination board, and may involve a simple short description or a more detailed PowerPoint or Prezi presentation. In addition, you will be required to outline the intentions of your research in information and consent letters. This will require a competency with information and communications technology (ICT). You are likely to need to design questionnaires and observation or interview schedules and to find an effective way of sharing your research findings with your research participants. You may find yourself communicating ideas in all sorts of formats, from a report to a letter to a leaflet or a poster. You will learn to present yourself clearly, engagingly and succinctly across a range of circumstances. Make sure that you include these new skills in your CV.

Communication and collaboration

As well as being able to communicate your ideas clearly, through some of the means mentioned above, you will also need to develop a range of collaborative working relationships. These will not only include connections with those in various posts of support at university (as discussed in Chapter 3), but will also include individuals at your place of research. If this is not a setting that you are already familiar with, then you will need to create trusting connections within a relatively short space of time. This will involve being very open and honest about the intentions of your research and demonstrating that you value both the time and the ideas of those whom you would like to ask to contribute to your research.

Critical analysis and reflection

There is a saying that is along the lines of 'Intelligence isn't about knowing everything, but about questioning everything that you know.' At postgraduate level, it is no longer enough to relate the 'what?' in your work without also exploring the 'why?' and the 'so what?' (see Chapter 5). During this time of study, you will not only have examined ideas in terms of the sociopolitical context (for example the implications of your study for policy in your field), and positioned them in relation to other emerging ideologies of the time, but you will have extended these ideas further. Your further reflection will have led you to the 'so what?' Why is this important? How does it relate to me and to my professional practice? And, better still, how might I further develop these ideas?

Whereas much of professional practice can be limited to accepting and acting on ideas and perhaps adapting these to your context, postgraduate study will have empowered you to question and to challenge rather than simply acquiescing.

Subject expertise

Whatever your postgraduate course has been, you will, by the end of your studies, have a certain degree of expertise in the area. As well as a good basic knowledge, you will also have looked into one particular area in some depth for a dissertation or for your doctoral research. You will have up-to-date knowledge about ideas and approaches that you will be able to share with your colleagues in order to further their professional development.

Research skills

By the conclusion of your degree, you will have carried out a piece of research. This will involve a number of skills that will prove useful in any field: working within professional ethical boundaries and designing information letters and permissions; designing an appropriate research approach which is suited to the research context and the aims of the research; selecting samples which will be purposive or representative of the whole; designing, piloting and redesigning data collection tools; and analysing and presenting data. Self-evaluation is now firmly embedded within all company and institute structures, therefore knowledge of suitable means of working with and sharing data will prove invaluable in your future job roles (Student Example 8.3).

Student example 8.3   Applying postgraduate research skills to work

Joe works for a graphic design company. He is an illustrator but took an MA in Leadership and Management as he was interested in starting up his own company. For his MA dissertation, he explored customer feedback systems. When his company heard about his research, they asked him to survey their own customers and design a relevant feedback system for them. As he was the only member of the company with research skills, they designed a research post especially for him and he is now called on for any project that involves information gathering.

He is still interested in running his own company, but the experience that he is currently gaining due to his postgraduate study, working with all departments of his company in an advisory capacity, is proving invaluable in preparation for that.

Confidence and resilience

Postgraduate study pushes you out of your comfort zone. It places you in new situations, where you will interact with a wide range of academics, professionals and practitioners. If you have been nervous about talking in front of an audience previously, then situations where you have to share your own ideas with academics who will question and challenge are likely to be terrifying for you. Be resilient: push yourself through these situations, because each time it will get easier. You will soon realise that everyone is nervous when they present (even seasoned entertainers still feel anxiety) – that is only natural. But with every presentation, and with every time you explain your research to a new acquaintance, the feelings of abject horror will subside. Being dumbstruck will simply become speaking a little too fast or stumbling over your words. It will become easier. And even though it may never actually become easy, you will realise the value of receiving feedback from fellow academics. Their questions and their challenges will enable to you to clarify and to further develop your ideas.

Researcher Development Framework (RDF)

The *Vitae* **Researcher Development Framework (RDF)** is a valuable resource for research students that has been developed by the Careers Research and Advisory Centre (CRAC). The RDF is structured into four domains that describe the knowledge, behaviours and attributes of researchers. Using this tool, research students can begin to map their own strengths and weaknesses and thus plan their personal development towards employment, whether in higher education or elsewhere (Drawing 8.1). The domains are:

- *Engagement, influence and impact*: The knowledge and skills to work with others and ensure the wider impact of research.
- *Knowledge and intellectual abilities*: The knowledge, intellectual abilities and techniques to do research.
- *Research governance and organisation*: The knowledge of the standards, requirements and professionalism to do research.
- *Personal effectiveness*: The personal qualities and approach to become an effective researcher.

Source: www.vitae.ac.uk/researchers-professional-development/about-the-vitae-researcher-development-framework (accessed 30 May 2017).

DRAWING 8.1   Doing personal development planning

Considering a teaching role in further education (FE) and higher education (HE)

A Master's degree or a PhD put you in an excellent position to apply for a teaching post at a college or university. You have now become an expert in your field and are in a position where you can pass your knowledge on as a tutor or lecturer. If this is an avenue that interests you, make sure to get some experience of teaching whilst completing your degree, if at all possible. If not, then take opportunities to shadow experienced lecturers and develop an understanding of approaches and systems within further education (FE) and higher education (HE). Most tutors would be more than happy to welcome you into their sessions. Although institutes will consider individuals with no teaching experience, gaining some experience will stand you in really good stead during the application process.

Further Study

It may be that you do not need to consider the ways in which your postgraduate degree will enhance your employability because your intention is to go on to further study. At one time, that would simply have meant completing an extended and significant piece of independent research over a number of years for a PhD, but now the options are more varied. You can pursue a doctorate on a full- or a part-time basis and you have the options of a taught doctorate, a doctorate by portfolio or the original, research-based route to a PhD (Student Example 8.4).

Student example 8.4   Doctorate choice: Practice or research

Makena has completed a Master's in Clinical Psychology and is unsure of which route to take to a PhD. There are two main options, a PhD in Psychology or a Psychology Doctorate (PsyD). From the information that she has gathered, a PhD in Psychology will require her to carry out her own, substantial piece of research. The aim of this will be to look into a relatively new area and to create new knowledge. Her role will be more as a researcher than a practitioner. Makena's real interest lies in her developing as an expert practitioner rather than as a scientist or an expert researcher.

Because of this, the PsyD seems to be a more appropriate route for Makena to take. This route has an emphasis on practice rather than research. Makena's future career goal is to develop her own consultancy business rather than to become an academic, therefore her interest is in becoming an expert in using and applying existing research rather than becoming an expert researcher.

All doctorates are equivalent, and are designated as Level 8 under the National Qualifications Framework for Higher Education in England, Wales and Northern Ireland. A doctorate is the highest level of degree that a student can achieve. All doctoral students are allocated a supervisor or Director of Studies by their university, and often there will be a supervisory team of two or three people who will each contribute their specialism in order to support the student's studies. The following gives a very brief overview of the different routes to achieving a doctorate.

Doctor of Philosophy or PhD

A Doctor of Philosophy or PhD will involve carrying out a significant piece of research in a specific subject. The aim is to produce by the end of the research an 80,000–100,000-word thesis that is of publishable quality. The thesis should offer a sound contribution to knowledge development. A full-time PhD will normally take about three to four years and a part-time route about six or seven years. Exact timings will be dependent on the institution and the influencing factors on the student. The PhD is examined by thesis and a viva examination. At Oxford University, this degree is termed a 'DPhil'.

Professional doctorate

Professional doctorates are growing in popularity, and generally exist in vocational areas such as Education (EdD), Management (DMan), Engineering (DEng) and Health (DHealth) rather than the Arts or Sciences. These degrees have a significant taught module component and require a smaller research project. They are frequently undertaken on a part-time basis and can last between two and eight years. They may well be taken alongside a current teaching role in a school, FE or HE or they may be taken by someone looking to become an expert in their vocation, such as a public sector manager, health practitioner or psychologist. Some universities offer a Doctorate in Professional Studies (DProf) that can be studied within any specialist professional field or sector. The professional doctorate still requires the student to contribute to the field of theory in their focus area, but the focus of this research will be the student's own professional practice. As well as the module assessments and dissertation mark, there will be an oral examination similar to the viva that PhD students undertake on submission of their thesis.

PhD by publication or portfolio

A PhD by publication or portfolio allows individuals who may not have followed a traditional route through education to reach their position of expertise, to receive recognition for the level of knowledge that they have developed, or for those who are already researching and publishing at doctoral level. The pieces of work selected have to be curated, brought into a coherent whole and set out with a significant explanatory introduction. The word requirement varies between disciplines. As well as the written portfolio of published work, as for the professional doctorate there will be an oral examination.

Developing an academic profile

If you consider your future to be based in academia, it is a good idea to develop your academic profile. Websites such as ResearchGate or LinkedIn provide opportunities for you to showcase your experience and expertise and to network with like-minded individuals. They can provide opportunities to profile your own work and identify potential new research partnerships and can even open up future job opportunities. These are definitely worth exploring. Blogs are another format used by a wide range of academics to share their ideas and their work. Hugh McGuire (2008) argues that blogs should be used by academics for a range of reasons, and these include:

- To improve your writing.
- To develop your ideas with the help of feedback from others.
- To share your knowledge more widely than the restricted readership of journals.
- To publish and thus protect your ideas.
- To develop your reputation.

The cyber world is not embraced by all, though, and this is certainly not the only way in which to share your knowledge and ideas.

Getting your work published

Getting your work published is a realistic ambition but requires careful thought and planning. Most important is to understand that the audience for a published output is different from the audience for a dissertation. That said, many dissertations are eminently publishable, reflecting as many do, months or years of dedicated thoughtful work in a specialist field that brings new knowledge into a discipline or professional field (Student Example 8.5).

Student example 8.5 Preparing part of your thesis as a journal article

Patrick is taking a PhD in Human Resource Management (HRM) in the Community and Voluntary sector, and wants to work up part of his thesis as a journal article. After reflecting on this, he decides to base an article on the six interviews that he carried out with Charity Chief Executive Officers (CEOs). In his research, he has identified a number of themes that the CEOs felt were crucial in making key staff appointments. He has been advised by his supervisor that since most journals specify a word limit of around 7000 words, he must be highly selective in drawing on his much longer thesis, and that there should be a distinct focus for the article. Patrick feels that the CEOs' reflections on ethics and sustainability would be appropriate for an article, and would engage a journal readership.

Patrick's article gives a short introduction to existing academic work in the field, paints the context of his research, briefly describes his methodology, and gives a selection of extracts from the interviews with each CEO, from which Patrick draws out the themes and ideas that have informed his thesis. The article thus contains sufficient information and evidence for readers to evaluate his work, without providing all the detail and background that was essential for his thesis. His title is short and to the point, and he lists the 20 or so references at the end of the article that he has cited to support his argument. He provides a 100-word abstract and six key words so as to enable students, academics and practitioners to find the article via a search engine, as required by the journal editors. He takes care to format his references in the 'Chicago author-date' style (from the *Chicago Manual of Style*), as specified in the journal's 'Guidelines for Contributors', which is different from the format required by his university for his PhD.

He then asks one of his tutors to act as a critical friend and read and comment on the article before he submits. His tutor helps Patrick to identify suitable management journals

(Continued)

that publish articles on HRM. She understands that academic journals require contributors to confirm that their article is not under active consideration by another publisher, so the choice of journal is an important one, since the refereeing process can take up to nine months before a decision is given to the author. Patrick is advised to check which journals have published work in his specialist field, and to look carefully at their aims and notes for contributors. Having selected several journals that seem to be a good fit, he then checks which of these has published most of the work that he has cited in his written work towards the PhD. One journal stands out after this screening process, and he feels confident in preparing an article for submission.

Most high-quality dissertations can, with a little imagination, be used as a source for an academic journal article. All will require adaptation and rewriting for the journal readership, so that the finished article will not read like an extract from a dissertation but will stand up by itself as a self-contained and coherent contribution to the field. A more challenging task, but entirely feasible, is to rewrite the academic project as a book. For those who are considering a career in higher education, getting a research-based book published gives a big advantage in the search for a lecturing or research post (Student Example 8.6).

Student example 8.6   Publishing your research as a book

Cosima is two years into a part-time EdD professional doctorate, in which she is undertaking a case study of the FE college where she holds the position of full-time Curriculum Director. She is interested in researching the career aspirations of the young people whom she teaches on a Business and Technology Education Council (BTEC) First Diploma in Health and Social Care. Through her reading of the literature and her professional knowledge and experience, she has developed a model of career choice that looks at the influence of family, friends, college tutors, work settings and media presentations. Her work and ideas build on other work that has been done in this area, but she believes that her model is original and adds to the theoretical literature on what influences career choice. She knows of three or four publishers who specialise in Health and Social Care, one of which has also launched a series on Careers Education. She downloads a book proposal form and researches other books in related areas and the potential market for her proposed book. She drafts out a chapter structure and a convincing rationale for the book, and identifies a number of professional associations and groups that would potentially be interested in buying it. Based on the drafts that she has completed so far for her EdD, she prepares two sample chapters, to be included with the book proposal. After sharing the proposal with a friend who is a published academic, and incorporating his helpful critical comments, Cosima sends in the completed proposal.

Both Student Example 8.5 and 8.6, as with all the others in this book, are based on real student experiences. Note, particularly, that both students in these examples make use of a qualified critical friend; this is a valuable way of developing as a writer of proposals, articles, chapters and books. Another common element to note is the value of detailed preparation and planning. In getting published, the selection of how and where to publish requires as much care and thought as does writing for academic purposes.

Preparing for the viva

The 'viva voce' examination, or **viva**, is a standard part of the assessment process for all doctoral-level qualifications, including professional doctorates and doctorate by publication or portfolio, as well as the traditional PhD route. Some Master's courses also incorporate a viva that can be part presentation and part question-and-answer session. The advice that we have given in this book for making academic presentations (see the section in Chapter 6 on 'Planning and Presenting Work Orally') applies equally to the viva, but the latter does require some special preparation in addition.

A key purpose of the viva is so that the examiners can satisfy themselves that the written work you have presented is actually your own work, and through the questions that they ask, and the answers that you provide, they will be able to make a simple judgement about that. So, it is obvious that part of the preparation needed for a viva is to read and reread your thesis carefully, and to make notes that you are able to use in the viva session itself. There are different ways of doing this, but one tried-and-tested method is to draw up an outline of all the chapters, and then make a list of all the key points that you have argued in each chapter, with their page numbers. Then, go through a printed copy of the thesis itself and highlight all of these key points so that you can easily refer to them when answering the examiners' questions. You may want to consider organising a practice viva with a friend or colleague who understands the subject field you are working in, as a way of familiarising yourself with being questioned on your thesis, structuring your key ideas and practising your responses.

The viva is also an opportunity for you to clarify any aspects of the thesis that the examiners have doubts about or that need explanation. This might be to explain why you have adopted a particular methodology and method (although, if you have followed the advice in this chapter, this should be made very clear in the thesis itself), or it might prepare you if perhaps the examiners want to ask you about other research and theories in your field that you might have drawn on or, alternatively, that might be missing from your work. It is the supervisor's or adviser's responsibility to try to ensure that the examiners who are selected are sympathetic to the approach that you have taken in your research and that they have adopted similar approaches in their own work, for example that they have used similar methodology themselves in their work such as qualitative research, and methods – for example case study. As the student, you are not allowed to play any part in the selection of the examiners, nor to have any prior contact with them, so you really are reliant on your supervisor's judgment in this.

In academia, we sometimes talk about the student 'defending' their thesis in a viva. This sounds a little scary, and a viva can be an uncomfortable two-hour experience, because, as in all academic or professional contexts, people's personalities and dispositions have a huge part to play and, if the emotional intelligences are out of alignment, then the conversations can be difficult. That said, we want to reassure you that in most cases, the examiners want you to do well and they will do their best to put you at your ease and give you every opportunity to give a good account of your research, why you have adopted your chosen approach, and what it is in your work that stands out and makes an original contribution to knowledge. Our advice is to create a set of 'stories' that demonstrate each of the elements that the examiners are looking for in assessing your work. To understand exactly what these elements are, go to your university website and search out the regulations for the degree that you are taking. The assessment criteria will be there, and it is these that you must demonstrate that you have achieved in your presentation and discussion with the examiners (Student Example 8.7).

Student example 8.7   Preparing an explanatory story for the viva

Becky is preparing for her PhD viva. She sees from the university PhD assessment criteria that one of the principal criteria is 'makes an original contribution to knowledge in the field'. She prepares one of her stories on this, highlighting how her work fits into the existing research in her field, how it supports the theoretical literature and how it extends that literature, thus showing originality. She also shows that no one has applied the theoretical approach that she has taken in the specific context in which she has located her work, again showing how the thesis establishes a fresh and novel dimension. Finally, her story includes a theoretical model that she has adapted from someone else's work (properly attributed and included in her 'List of References', of course), but that adds some new features that arise from her own data. Becky's story gives a convincing account of her original contribution to the theoretical literature, and the examiners find it clear and compelling.

The rule is to make the job as easy as you can for the examiners, and they will be delighted to conclude that you are worthy of becoming an academic doctor.

Key ideas and terms

Intercalation is taking a break from your studies, which may be for a variety of reasons, including domestic, health or work pressures.

Emotional support is recognised as a vital part of student services in all universities, and is available to everyone in order to help them deal with personal and work difficulties, and is an important dimension of peer support and friendships.

Mitigating circumstances, or 'mit circs', are formal university procedures to deal with extending deadlines and below par assessment performance due to some intervening personal or health issues.

Complaints procedures are in place in all universities and are designed to protect students from unfair or unsatisfactory treatment, whatever the source.

Employability is increasingly a core aspect of higher education, preparing students for work through placements, work-based projects, and a range of relevant learning and skills.

Critical analysis and reflection are central to high-level postgraduate performance, involving going beyond the 'what?' in your work to exploring the 'why?' and the 'so what?'

Research skills are an invaluable asset to take into employment and wider life, including self-evaluation, which is now firmly embedded in all organisational structures.

The **Researcher Development Framework (RDF)** is structured into four domains that describe the knowledge, behaviours and attributes of researchers. Using this tool, research students can begin to map their own strengths and weaknesses and thus plan their personal development towards employment, whether in higher education or elsewhere.

Professional doctorates are available in many vocational subjects and provide an alternative route to a doctorate other than a traditional PhD by research. They are usually made up of a combination of taught modules and a shorter research dissertation element.

Journal articles can be sourced from dissertations or thesis chapters, but careful thought and adaptation is necessary to ensure that the work is appropriate for the journal readership.

The **viva** examination enables examiners to check that the dissertation is your own work and to clarify any areas that they need to explore with you. For you, it is an opportunity to present 'stories' that demonstrate each of the elements that the examiners are looking for in assessing your work

Chapter summary

This chapter focuses on the support that you may call on as a postgraduate student and the opportunities that can follow on from postgraduate study. Both academic and emotional support are widely available in UK universities, and no student should feel that they have to battle on alone without being able to seek advice and help. University regulations allow for extensions to deadlines and compensation for poor performance where there is an overriding personal circumstance or problem, as well as opportunities to take a break from studies where that is needed. The benefits of postgraduate study for employability are detailed, including how it can develop learning and skills for independent study, time management, presentations, communication and collaboration, critical analysis and reflection, subject expertise, research skills, confidence and resilience. Guidance is given for those at Master's level who wish to pursue a doctorate, and for those considering a lecturing career. We advise on developing an academic profile, and on converting dissertations and thesis chapters into academic journal articles and books. Finally, we explain the purpose of the viva exam and how to prepare for it.

References

Crossley, M. (undated) *Planning and Writing a Dissertation: Working with Your Adviser*. Bristol: Graduate School of Education, University of Bristol.

Engeström, Y. (2001) 'Expansive learning at work: Toward an activity theoretical conceptualisation', *Journal of Education and Work*, 14 (1): 133–56.

Luca, M. (2009) 'Embodied research and grounded theory'. Available at: www.regents.ac.uk/media/611246/Article-for-Research-centre1-Dr-M-Luca-2009.pdf (accessed 28 October 2015).

McGuire, H. (2008) 'Why academics should blog', *The Huffington Post*. Available at: www.huffingtonpost.com/hugh-mcguire/why-academics-should-blog_b_138549.html (accessed 15 May 2017).

McNiff, J. (2010) *Action Research for Professional Development*. Dorset: September Books.

Stebbing, L.S. (1939) *Thinking to Some Purpose*. Harmondsworth: Penguin Books.

Index

Abstract, 81–83, 119
Academic
area, 48–49
  argument, 62–64, 69
  books, 49
  development, 37
  English, 73, 77
  etiquette, 29–42
  integration, 66–67
  language, 56, 71–73, 85–86
  profile, 118–119
  support, 1, 30, 73, 108–109
  reflection, 57
  texts, 49, 55, 64, 75, 85
  tutor, 33, 67
  writer(s), 52, 64
  writing, 56–57, 61–62, 69, 76, 85–87
Acknowledgements, 81
Acquisition, 73–74
Acronyms, 76
Administrator, 36
Admissions tutor, 16. 27
Aim(s), 18, 53, 78–79, 92–95, 102–104, 114, 117, 120
Allowance, 110
Analysis, 20, 39, 57, 61–62, 68, 73, 80–93, 113
  analysing, 62, 73
  analytical, 56, 61
  content, 93, 97
  critical, 82, 112, 123
  statistical, 62, 94–95
Anonymity, 99
Application(s), 7, 16, 27, 69, 116
  statement, 16
Applying to university, 15–28
Apps, 13
Argument(s), 45, 50, 56–65, 69, 73–85
  arguing,70, 73–74, 84
  effective, 61–62
Article(s), 7, 8, 12, 27, 44–48, 50–58, 64–65, 73, 82–83, 119–121, 123

Assessment(s), 4, 9, 11, 21, 23, 28, 36, 38, 61, 63, 67, 68, 74, 80, 84, 110, 118, 121–123
Assignment, 5, 9, 12–13, 20, 25, 34, 44–55, 59–61, 68, 80–81
  deadlines, 11–12
Assumptive world of the researcher, 100
Audience(s), 56–57, 62–64, 69, 72, 75–83, 86, 113, 115, 119

Back up copy, 54–55
Bereavement, 107
Bias, 99
Blog, 46, 48, 55, 66, 82, 118
Body of knowledge, 55, 63
Book proposal, 120
  bookshop, 26
British Council, 7
Burnout, 40

Case,
  selection, 80
  study, 4, 58, 65, 68, 90–97, 104, 120, 122
Childcare, 107
Choosing a course, 7, 18, 20, 27
Clarity, 16, 64, 75–76, 78
Classroom, 4, 38, 74
Co-author, 40
Collaboration, 20, 37, 112–113
Communication, 32, 35, 41, 113
Complaint(s), 111, 123
Comprehension, 76
Computer, 39–40, 55, 65, 85
Conceptual framework, 53, 55
Conference, 48, 55, 73, 83
  paper, 83
Conclusion, 61, 63, 80
  concluding, 73, 84
Confidence, 1, 5, 8, 12, 35, 71, 79, 92, 112, 115
  crisis of, 107–108
  confidentiality, 99

Consistency,112
   internal, 61, 69
Constructivism, 94–95
   constructivist, 40, 95, 98, 104
Contents,
   Table of, 102
Context, 7, 9, 15, 29, 41, 56, 60–61, 66,
   70, 78, 85, 88, 102, 104, 113, 114,
   119, 122
   contextual, 74,
   contextualisation, 69
   contextualise, 60–61, 97, 102
Copyright, 41
Counsellors, 109–110
Course,
   choosing a, 16, 20
   handbook, 32–33
   representative (rep), 35
   leader, 35
   management committee, 67
Crisis, 34, 107, 108
Critical,
   analysis, 82, 112, 113, 123
   criticality, 56, 60–61, 65
   friend, 76, 119, 121
   perspectives, 58
   reader, 9, 51, 63, 69
   reflection, 57
   stance, 62, 69, 74
   theory, 53, 95
   thinking, 44, 82
Criticism, 37, 61
   criticising, 73
Culture, 7, 89, 107
   cultural influences 6, 13
CV, 111, 113

Data, 17, 40, 53–55, 62–65, 80, 95, 97, 100, 104,
   114, 122
database, 100
Deadline, 6, 10–12, 34, 36, 100, 123
Decision-making, 18, 74, 112
DEng, 117
Descriptive, 57, 61, 95
Desk environment, 37
Device(s), 55, 79, 85, 86
DHealth, 117
Dialogue, 30, 57, 68, 83
Dictionary, 69
Difficult, 6, 32, 38, 52, 81, 85, 108–109, 122
   difficulties, 22, 26, 34–35, 44, 110, 123
   difficulty, 81
Discourse, 68, 71–73, 79–80, 85–87

Discussion(s), 29, 38, 40, 62, 80, 82, 90, 96, 98,
   99, 104, 122
   boards, 38
Dissemination, 82, 84–85
Dissertation (see also Thesis), 4, 25, 36, 45, 47,
   51–53, 62, 64, 65–67, 79, 81, 88–105, 107,
   119–120, 123
Distinction, 4, 36
DMan, 117
Doctorate, 16, 24–25, 57, 82, 116–123
   by publication, 118, 121
   by portfolio, 116, 118
   professional, 117–118, 120–121, 123
   taught, 116
DProf, 118
Draft, 30, 55, 64, 68, 73–77, 79, 80, 85, 88, 90,
   101–103, 120
Duty of care, 99, 104
Dyslexia, 108

EAP, see English for Academic Purposes,
Earn as you learn, 15, 23–26, 28
EdD, 24, 66, 117, 120
Eloquent, 75
Email, 30, 31, 34, 109
Emotional support, 109, 123
Employment, 16–17, 27–28, 106–107,
   115, 123
   employability, 17–18, 21, 26, 111–112,
   116, 123
EndNote, 103
English,
   for Academic Purposes (EAP), 72–73, 80,
   83–84, 86
Enjoying university, 21, 28
Essay, 9, 12, 55, 58, 61–62, 64, 65, 74, 77–79,
   81, 85, 113
   plan, 61
Ethics, 67, 69, 98–100, 119
   ethical approval, 59, 88, 98
Ethnography, 97, 104
Etiquette, 29–42
Evaluate(d) 59, 119
   Evaluative, 56
Evidence 2, 6, 9, 14, 54, 57–58, 61–65, 69, 76,
   91, 110, 119
   -based research, 62
Expectations, 6, 30, 37, 41, 80
Experience(s) (d), 1–7, 16–28, 37, 51, 53, 56, 60,
   62, 67–68, 88, 95, 98, 100, 104, 118, 120
   learning, 38, 51
   student, 21, 121
   work, 15, 17, 26, 116

Expert(s), 6, 35, 40, 49, 72, 73–74, 80, 81, 82,
    95, 107, 108, 117, 118
    expertise, 22, 35, 38, 41, 74, 90, 108, 112,
        114, 118
Eye contact, 78–79

Face-to-face, 33–34, 38
FE (see Further education colleges),
Feedback, 30, 33, 64, 67, 68, 74, 82, 114,
    115, 118
Fees, 23–25, 108
Field, 9, 27, 35, 39, 46, 54, 73–74, 82, 86, 91, 93,
    96, 103, 106, 113–122
    notes, 39
    of enquiry, 75, 86
    of study, 44, 49, 65
    work, 39
Figures of speech, 79
Filing, 7, 53
Finance, 5, 22, 35–36, 107, 108
    financial help, 108
First person, 76
Forest to leaf, 70
Formative, 68, 80, 81
'For profit' institution, 23
Frames of reference, 57
Framework of Higher Education
    Qualifications, 16
Full-time, 11, 15, 16–19, 22–25, 39, 117
Functional system, 72, 84, 86
Further education colleges, 22
Further study, 37, 116

Gantt chart, 101
Glossaries, 74
Google, 48, 65, 102
Grade, 8, 11, 33, 36, 44, 54, 57, 68, 77, 81
Grammar, 71, 72, 76, 84
Guidelines for contributors, 82, 119

Headings, 102
Health, 5, 21, 23, 25, 65, 73, 76, 80, 87, 89,
    95–96, 97. 107, 110, 117–118, 120, 123
    mental, 39, 107, 110
    physical, 110
Heath and Care Professions Council, 23
Hedging, 72, 86
Hermeneutic – see Paradigm,
Higher Education and Research Act 2017,
    22, 23
High level research question, 66, 70
Highlighting, 50, 51
Holistic, 61, 69
Hook, 78, 80, 86
Humour, 78

ICT, 113
Identity, 60
Illness, 6, 34, 101, 109, 110
Illumination, 37
Imagination, 120
Imposter syndrome, 4–5, 13, 106
Independent
    student, 67
    study, 17, 112
Information 5, 8, 14, 23, 28, 30, 32, 37–39, 41,
    50, 58, 67, 72, 79, 83, 85, 99, 100, 105, 113,
    114, 117, 119,
Informed consent, 99, 104
Integrity, 60–61, 63
    integrative perspective, 59
Intellectual property right, 41
Intention(s), 73, 77, 83–84, 86
Intercalate, 36, 107–108, 110, 123
Internal consistency, 61
International
    conference, 83
    student, 6–7, 21, 73
Interpretivist, 53, 55, 95
Introduction, 1–2, 61, 78, 80, 82, 100, 118, 119
    introducing, 73, 78, 84
IPR – see Intellectual property right,
Iterative, 90, 93

Jargon, 75–76
Journal, 48, 57, 62, 64, 82–83, 85
    article, 44, 47, 50, 58, 119–120, 123
    special issue, 48, 55

Key term, 49, 55, 59–60, 65–66, 69–70, 74, 77
Knowledge, 4–5, 9, 17, 25, 35–38, 40–41, 49,
    50–55, 58, 63, 65, 67, 72, 74–76, 79, 82–86,
    89, 91, 94–97, 100, 103, 114–123

Learner, 3–14, 20, 51, 66
Learning,
    outcomes, 5, 80
    representation of, 57, 68
    styles, 8, 13
Lecture(s), 11, 48, 64, 66, 79
Lens(es), 57, 66
Level 4/8, 16, 56
Lexis, 72, 73
Librarian, 26, 27 35–36, 49–50, 52, 55, 96, 108
Library, 7, 8, 12, 15, 26–27, 32, 35–36, 40,
    49–50, 55, 65, 68
Linguistic skills, 71–87
LinkedIn, 118
Literary device(s), 79
Literature,
    grey, 47, 49, 52, 54, 58, 65, 96, 102

policy, 43, 90, 94, 96, 97, 103
review, 40, 47, 53, 54, 80, 94, 96
search, 47, 49, 54, 55, 65
theoretical, 27, 36, 43, 52–53, 55, 92–98, 103, 104, 120, 122
Loan(s), 18, 25, 108
inter-library, 36

MA, 22, 23, 36, 40, 114
Magazine, 57–58
Marker(s), 61, 80
Mastery, 89
Meditation, 4, 6, 12–14
Mentor, 35, 57
Meta function(s), 72–73, 84–86
Metaphor(s), 9, 44, 54, 66, 70, 79
Methodology,
qualitative, 94–95, 97, 104
quantitative, 62, 94–95, 97, 104
Mind, 5–6, 11, 12–13, 57
maps, 8–9, 14, 63
Mindfulness, 4, 12–14
Mistake(n), 38, 77, 97
Mitigating circumstance ('mit circs'), 6, 110, 123
Mock audience, 64
Mode of study, 20
Moderate, 80
Module(s), 5, 9, 15, 17, 18, 20, 25–28, 43–49, 52–55, 80–81, 107
guide, 11
outline, 30, 32
resource list, 26, 47, 49, 52, 55
taught, 29, 37, 117, 123
tutor, 26, 32, 80
MRes, 17
Multilingual, 59–60

National Qualifications Framework for higher education (NQF), 18, 117
National student survey (NSS), 21, 23
Needs, 3, 5, 7, 35, 60, 69, 108
NHS, 77–78, 90, 92, 93, 99
Nomenclature, 73, 74, 84, 86
Nominalisation, 77–78, 86
Note taking, 50–51
NQF – see National Qualifications Framework for higher education,
NSS – see National student survey,

Objective(s), 13, 53, 78, 79, 92–94, 96, 102, 104
Observing self, 12–14
Office for Standards in Education (OfSTED), 23
Office of the Independent Adjudicator (OIA), 111

OfSTED – see Office for Standards in Education,
Online, 6, 13, 17, 19, 27–28, 38, 49–50, 55, 64, 66, 68, 71, 102
Open day, 22, 28
Open University, 19, 52
Oral
examination, 82, 118
oracy, 72
presentation, 63–64, 78–79, 80–81
Organisation,
researching in, 4, 99–100
skills, 93, 112, 115
Overview, 45, 50, 52, 80
of the study, 47, 54, 88, 92, 100, 102

Panic, 108
Paradigm, 94–98, 103, 104
Paragraph, 51, 71, 75, 84, 85
Parameter(s), 60, 63, 69
Participants, 37, 39, 62, 88, 95, 98–100, 104, 109, 113
Part-time, 1, 11, 15, 18–19, 22, 24, 25–26, 36, 108, 116, 117–118, 120
Peer(s), 29, 41, 52, 57, 81, 83, 112–113, 123
group support, 19, 20, 123
learning, 37–39, 68
Permission, 99–100, 114
Personal biography, 16
PGCE, 18, 25, 111
PhD, 17, 22, 23, 40, 41, 66, 111, 116–119, 122, 123
by publication or portfolio, 118, 121
Platitudes, 58, 68
Policy documents, 47, 58, 65
Polishing, 75, 77, 85
Positionality, 57
Positivism, 94–95
Poster, 113
Potted thinking, 44–45, 51, 54
Power, 12, 14, 95, 99
PowerPoint, 4, 78–79, 113
Practice, 17, 56, 58–59, 63–64, 74, 89, 90, 92–96, 113–114,117–118
Practitioner, 57, 65, 115, 117, 119
Pragmatics, 72, 84, 86
Pregnancy, 107
Premise, 61–62, 63, 69
Premodifiers, 77, 86
Presentation, 1–2, 4–5, 8–9, 12, 20, 64, 69, 78–81, 83–84, 115, 120, 121–122,
skills, 112–113
Pre-sessional courses, 21, 73
Prezi, 79, 113
Private providers, 31

Procrastination, 10
Production schedule, 100–102
Professional(s), 25, 30, 32, 44, 58, 64, 65, 75, 83,
    86–87, 97
  body and association, 96, 103, 120
  communication, 41
  course, 17–18, 19
  development, 17, 18, 98
  doctorate, 117–118, 120, 121, 123
  field and contexts, 91, 118–119, 122
  knowledge and experience, 16, 18, 88, 89, 92,
    94, 100, 102–103, 104, 120
  practice, 59, 74, 89, 90, 113–114, 118
  professionalism, 32, 115
  qualification, 19
  standards, 102
  studies, 18, 21, 23, 41, 76, 80, 94, 102
Programme (see course),
Project, 8, 12, 15, 17, 20, 41, 65, 109, 114,
    120, 123
Proposal, 88–105, 120–121
Publish(ed), 40–41, 48, 81–85, 118, 119–121
  publication, 40–41, 81–82, 106
  publishable, 75, 117
Punctuation, 75, 77
  punctuating devices, 79

QAA – see Quality Assurance Agency for
    Higher Education (QAA),
Quality Assurance Agency for Higher
    Education (QAA), 21, 23
Qualitative, 40, 62, 95, 122,
  research methodology, 95, 97, 98, 104
Quantitative, 62, 95
  research methodology, 94–95, 97, 104
Question(s), 4, 5, 20, 38, 53, 60–62, 66, 68, 70,
    79, 80, 82, 83, 89, 90, 93, 94, 96, 99, 103,
    115, 121
  questionnaire, 94, 97, 100, 104, 113
Quotation, 62

Rationale, 62, 91–92, 98, 120
Read, 57, 75–76, 82, 90, 121
  meta, meso, and micro reading, 45–47, 50, 54
  reader(s), 15, 52, 58, 59, 61–69, 71, 76, 79, 89,
    91–92, 104
  readership, 85, 118–120, 123
  reading, 1, 12, 26–27, 28, 39, 43–55, 58, 72,
    73, 77, 79, 94, 110
Recommended texts, 45
REF – see Research Excellence Framework,
References, 44–48, 51, 53–54, 61, 89, 100, 102,
    103, 119, 122
  list of, 81, 122
  referencing, 35, 61, 79, 82

Reflection, 56–57, 65, 73, 82, 84, 86, 112,
    113–114, 119, 123
  reflecting, 5, 12, 14, 38, 65, 73, 119
  reflective 'I', 57–58, 68, 76
Register, 6, 35–36
Registry, 22, 36
Rehearse, 64, 69, 78–79
Relationship(s), 29–30, 34–36, 39–40,
    99–100, 113
  problems, 107
Repetition, 79
Rephrasing, 79
Report, 23, 49, 53–54, 58, 59, 65, 94–95, 99, 102
  reporting, 73, 82
Represent(ing), 57
  representation, 56, 57, 68
Research Excellence Framework (REF), 21, 23
Research, 57–58, 62, 65–66, 70, 82, 84, 89,
    91–93, 99–100, 109, 112–113, 117, 120, 122
  assistant, 41
  degree, 1, 89, 104
  enquiry, 68
  question(s), 53, 66, 70, 80, 93–94, 96, 103
  literature, 1, 69, 91, 96–97, 103, 109
  method, 62, 65–66, 94–98, 101, 104, 121–122
  methodology, 47, 94–95, 97–98, 104
  researcher, 99–100
  skills, 112, 114, 123
  student, 1, 17, 22, 31, 36, 37, 39, 109,
    115, 123
  supervision, 34
  techniques/instruments, 97, 104
  work-based, 48, 100
Researcher Development Framework (RDF),
    111, 115, 123
ResearchGate, 118
Resilience, 112, 115
  and perseverance, 11–12, 14
Resource list, 26, 28, 44, 47, 49, 55
Rhetoric, 79

Saving, 53–54
Scaffolding, 8–9, 14
SCONUL, 27
Script, 79
Search engine, 35, 65, 68, 119
Self, 12–14
  evaluation, 114, 123
  management, 47
Semantics, 72, 76, 84–86
Seminar(s), 66–67
Semi-structured interview, 97–98, 104
Sense(s), 57
Sentence, 51, 64, 74–78, 84, 85
Setbacks, 106

Shared enterprise, 63, 69
Signposting, 50, 78
Skills, 1, 5, 9, 12, 16, 18, 20, 51, 56, 64, 67–68,
    71–87, 93, 111–115, 123
Solecism, 77
Speech(es), 64, 72
SPSS, 40
Stating, 72–73, 84, 85
Statistics, 40, 60, 62
    statistical analysis, 62, 94–95
Stress, 4–5, 13, 26
Structure, 4, 11, 47, 56, 59–64, 69, 78–81, 86,
    89, 102, 120
    structured development, 61, 63, 69
    structured interview, 97–98, 104
Student,
    charter, 35
    services, 5, 11, 35, 68, 109, 111, 123
    support, 6, 68
Students' union, 5, 17, 22, 35, 111
Stupid, 38
Study skills, 67–68
Stylistic, 57, 76
Subject expertise, 112, 114
    librarian, 26–27, 35–36, 49–50, 52, 55, 96
Summon, 49
Supervisor(s), 1, 16, 33, 67, 82, 99, 104, 108,
    1171, 119, 121–122
    supervisory team, 29, 117
Support,
    academic, 1, 30, 73, 108
    emotional, 109–110, 123
    writing, 108
Surface function, 84, 85
Survey(s), 21, 23, 28, 94, 97, 104, 114
Syntax, 84–85
Synthesis(ing), 72–74, 82, 84, 86

Talk, 20, 35, 37, 52, 64, 67–68, 78–79,
    107–110, 115
Teacher, 6, 13, 18, 23, 30, 40, 97, 111
Teaching Excellence Framework (TEF), 21, 23
Team, 33, 41, 90–96, 117
TED online lectures, 64
TEF – see Teaching Excellence Framework,
Text, 7, 26, 32, 41, 45, 50, 52, 61, 69, 73–78,
    84–85, 88
Theoretical, 13, 20, 54, 82, 91–92, 103
    framework, 53, 55, 80, 94, 97, 104
    literature, 27, 36, 43, 52–53, 55, 90, 92–94,
        96, 98, 103, 104, 120, 122
    orientation, 103
Theorising, 59, 68, 69, 84

Theory, 9, 25, 53, 55, 90, 95, 118
    and practice, 16–17, 20, 94
Thesis (see also Dissertation), 47, 62, 64, 66,
    69, 81–82, 83, 84, 88–105, 107, 117–119,
    121–122, 123
    theses, 64, 69, 102
Thinking, 4, 12, 13, 18, 37, 38, 43–45, 51, 54,
    56–70, 74, 82
Third person, 76
Third spaces, 37
Time, 7, 12, 33–34, 38, 41, 45, 76, 83, 88,
    100–102, 110
    management, 29, 39–40, 89, 112
    out, 40
    table, 39, 100–101, 112
Title, 49, 59, 60, 61, 68, 90, 119
Topic, 8–9, 14, 27, 45–50, 52–55, 58, 61, 64–65,
    88–92, 103, 104
Transformative paradigm – see critical theory,
Trust, 39, 41
Tutor(s), 16, 30, 31–38, 40–41, 45, 64, 68, 81,
    88, 90, 102, 104, 108–111, 116
    academic, 33, 67
    admissions, 16, 27
    module, 32, 80
    personal, 35, 64
    tutorial, 5, 34, 64, 68, 74, 80, 99, 109, 112

University(ies), 3–7, 15–28, 35, 67, 111, 116, 123
    library, 26–28, 49–50, 102

Virtual learning environment (VLE), 32
Viva, 82, 117–118, 121–123
VLE – see Virtual learning environment,
Volunteering, 17, 21, 22

Web, 47–49
    site, 16, 23, 82, 118, 122
Wikipedia, 50, 57
Word(s), 9, 27, 55, 58, 60, 65, 73, 75–79, 82, 84,
    117–119
    Microsoft, 102–103
    processing, 50
Work, 1, 4, 15, 19, 22, 25–26, 28, 66, 91, 98,
    111–114
    based learning, 11, 15, 28, 90
    based research, 48, 100
    experience, 15, 17, 89
    paid, 11, 26
    place, 88–89, 90, 99
Working title, 90
Writing, 1, 9, 14, 27–28, 39, 43, 56–58, 60–69,
    81–87, 89, 93–94, 98, 101, 118